MAKEUP COLORS

EYESHADOWS

gold   russet   silver   clear blue   turquoise

yellow   peach   taupe   olive   bronze

rose-gold   lavender   magenta   royal   mauve

SHADOW/LINERS

black   brown   gray   navy   plum

sage   dark teal   dark olive   purple   breen (brown-green)

BLUSHERS

buff pink   coral   fuschia   beige rose   contour

LIPSTICKS

pink   fuschia   coral   clear red   orange   rosy tan

The H-O-A-X *Fashion Formula*

The H-O-A-X Fashion Formula

DRESS THE BODY TYPE YOU HAVE
TO LOOK LIKE THE BODY YOU WANT

by MARY DUFFY

Illustrations by GABRIELLE BOSTROM

Photographs by MICHAEL MARKIW

Hairstyles by Glemby Salons • Makeup by Deborah Steele

THE BODY PRESS
Tucson, Arizona

© 1987 Mary Duffy

Designed by Helen Barrow

Published by
THE BODY PRESS
A division of HPBooks, Inc.
575 East River Road
Tucson, Arizona 85704

ISBN 0-89586-581-5
Printed in U.S.A.
1st Printing
10 9 8 7 6 5 4 3 2 1

All photographs by Michael Markiw except where indicated.

Library of Congress Cataloging in Publication Data

Duffy, Mary, 1945-
   The H O A X fashion formula.

   1. Beauty, Personal.   2. Clothing and dress.
3. Cosmetics.   4. Hairdressing.   I. Title.
II. Title: Hoax fashion formula.
   RA778.D885   1987   646.7'042   87-741
   ISBN 0-89586-581-5

To Mom and Dad

and

to the memory of Aunt Gert and Stanley

ACKNOWLEDGMENTS

To Derek, Audrey and Virginia

To those who worked so hard on this book:
Anne Allison • Judith Wesley Allen • Roy Baxter • Gabrielle Bostrom • Brigitte Grosjean • Marilyn Hawkridge • Faith Hornby • Michael Markiw • Susan Milano • Rita Milo • Randy Royer • Greta Sokoloff • Deborah Steele

To the models of Big Beauties who contributed their photographs and time for this book—especially those models who posed for unflattering *don'ts*, putting away vanity to prove a point:
Alex • Christine Alt • Jodi Applegate • Pat Barker • Karla Brown • Jeannie Brown • Ruth Button • Virginia DeBerry • Liz Dillon • Colleen Flynn-Lawson • Amy Geary • Meg Giannotti • Donna Grant • Jennifer Holmes • Kaitlynn • Kathleen MacKenzie • Gail Malis • Martha • Sally Morgan • Lyne Pedola • Audrey Preston • Rae • Mo Roberts • Tara Robinson • Liliana Santini • Lucinda Shankle • Darcy Slavin • Carolyn Strauss • Lill Thompson • Teri White • Karen Wright • Diane Wyda

To our wonderful clients who contributed merchandise and services for the photos, expecially:
CET • Danskin • Gemini • Givenchy • Gitano • Hanes • Joske's • Nipon • Royal Woman • Russ • Schrader • Young Stuff

To my friends who have been so encouraging over the years, especially those who were so supportive while I was writing under a difficult deadline:
Carin & Ed • Art • Jan & Bill • Sally • John M. • Joe • John W. • Pat & Fabyn • Lynn • Jackie & Dan • C.J. • Bill M. • Peter • Bill B. • Alan

To those who were so helpful at the beginning of Big Beauties and my career, for which I have been so grateful:
Carol Nashe • Renee Bond • Debra Kalscheur • Ken Talberth • Sean O'Brien

CONTENTS

Contents

1

You Are What You Are. Make the Most of It!

Dedication

> This book is dedicated to every woman who has ever felt flawed in comparison to the young, bone-thin, drop-dead-beautiful "perfect woman" image projected by:
>
> - Madison Avenue ads
> - The world of "vogue" fashion
> - Celebrity fitness gurus
> - Weight-watching, profit-making organizations
>
> This book is further dedicated to every woman who is any of the following:
>
> - Short
> - Tall
> - Average sized (10 to 16)
> - Large sized (18 and over)
> - Not built like Raquel Welch
> - Not likely to be the next Miss America
>
> In short, this book is dedicated to *real women*.

FOR YEARS I have had a friend whom I (and everyone else) considered very good-looking. One day a man who had just met her commented that he liked her very much and was very impressed by the way she put herself together, considering that she was rather homely. I was shocked—all the more so when I looked at her and realized it was true. My friend knew how to *present* herself in the most *positive* way, and we all found her very attractive.

In an ideal world people would judge us on our internal beauty. Unfortunately this is not an ideal world and people's first judgment of us frequently proceeds from their impression of our physical presentation. I use the work "presentation" in the same way it is used in gourmet cooking. The way we dress, groom and carry ourselves is window dressing that is as important to our relationships with others as packaging is to product marketing.

In my business I know many beautiful women from size 4 to size 24. They know that it is not what you've got or how much, but what you do with it that counts. The fashion, beauty, success, happiness and romance game is for everyone.

Today I can walk into any department store and spot at fifty paces an article of clothing that is perfect for me. This is no idle boast but a matter of fact. It has been years since I made a fashion mistake, because I know what is appropriate for me in terms of body type, coloring and style. Today, at 41, I look and dress the best in my life, do not spend a fortune on clothes, and am considered one of the best-dressed women in my industry.

I frequently pick out clothes for my friends and travel for department stores about 20 percent of the year, telling women all over the country how to dress and look their best. By the time you finish reading this book, you will have the skills to do these same things for yourself. You will know exactly what is right for you.

I am, today, happy and sure of myself. For years, however, I was a fashion and beauty victim. How did this change occur? Through knowledge and confidence I acquired from talking to women all over the country (I am a busy fashion-show commentator) and hearing how they feel about fashion, beauty, attitudes, roles and life in general.

Over the years, I have formulated a simple but thorough fashion and beauty program which my clients

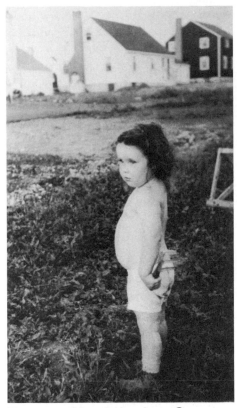

Two years old and already an O

have come to call my H-O-A-X Formula. This formula prescribes the best possible physical presentation of each woman in terms of five elements:

1. Body type
2. Coloring
3. Lifestyle
4. Personality
5. Grooming needs

The H-O-A-X Formula began as a body-type analysis. The name H-O-A-X comes from the four basic female shapes, each of which resembles a letter:

H = The straight up and down figure
O = The full middle-torso figure
A = The full-hip-and-thigh figure
X = The hourglass figure

The H-O-A-X Formula has now evolved into a positive, make-the-most-of-what-you've-got philosophy evolving from the *double-entendre* of the acronym formed by the letters H-O-A-X. To me, the biggest hoax of life for modern women is that for each gain we have made in social status, we have found new ways to put ourselves down for physical imperfections. Even the term "imperfections" (or the fashion favorite "figure flaws") is a put-down—I prefer the term "figure realities."

Throughout this book I will be describing the best and worst looks for each H-O-A-X figure type as part of the H-O-A-X philosophy. But first, I would like to tell you about my background and how the H-O-A-X Formula came to be.

THE ABBREVIATED SOAP OPERA OF MY LIFE OR A SMALL, SAD STORY WITH A BIG, HAPPY ENDING

(Violin music . . .) I was a pretty, healthy, well-adjusted child and teenager with a keen interest in breakfast, lunch and dinner—and a distinct tendency toward chubbiness. A popular, good student all through school, I went on my first diet at age 11 and was a

*Junior prom (1961): a 26-inch
waist and feeling fat*

*Graduation photo (1966):
125 pounds for 5 minutes*

calorie-counting pro by high school. By the time I graduated from college, food and slimness had become mutually exclusive, four-star obsessions at odds with each other. A tornado was brewing inside of me and a part of my self-esteem was on a miserable course.

A big eater from babyhood, I had nevertheless bought the notion that on the personal worth, happiness and marriage markets of life, I was valuable inversely by the pound. Weight would determine whether my label was "sold to the highest bidder" or "markdown rack."

What I ate on any given day determined how I felt about myself in all areas of my life. My weight even affected my love relationships.

Throughout my twenties, I dated a great deal and had several opportunities for marriage. Every time I came close to making a real commitment, however, I would enter a classic "approach-avoidance" conflict. On one hand, I felt a desire to be independent, admired and respected for my own worth. On the other hand, I wanted love and protection and felt that marriage would prove my worth. When my come-here-and-go-away behavior would finally end a relationship, I would blame my weight and go on a crash diet. I would console myself by saying, "If I lose 15 pounds, everything will be fine." To say the least, I was confused.

Further ambivalence came from my image of a woman's role in marriage. I had read Betty Friedan and felt too bright and educated to devote my life to routine housework. At the same time, I felt totally inadequate to the demands for consistency and discipline that I perceived in my mother and other women I saw as "proper wives." Recently I found an essay I had written for the *Mademoiselle* magazine College Board that reflected my idea of what a woman should do. It said:

"I'd rather do something with my life, but I'm fighting it—after all, I'm a woman—I don't have to do anything. Someone else can take care of the world, while I sit back, being a huge success as a traditional woman. I can go back to bed after breakfast.

"Choice is for men? Women belong in the home?"

The year was 1963, and while I had never heard the

24 years old and losing my waistline

expression "emerging feminist rage," that is exactly where my confusion would lead. It was all very black and white to me then—I could be useful and productive or I could be dependent and protected. I had no idea that I could be both and was afraid to commit to either.

I dwelled on my moderate overweight instead (a bad solution to conflict: ignore it and fixate on some less-important issue). I was also furious to think that so much of my value as a woman was dependent on my physical appearance. Wasn't it enough, I thought, to be witty, bright, educated, warm, loving and a size 14? When people said, "Mary, you have such a pretty face. If only . . ." I was shamed and hurt to a state of near panic—and the panic triggered some desperate and pathetic courses of action.

By the time I was 30 I had been through bulimia, diet pills (and of course tranquilizers), exercise clubs, diuretics, fads, fasts, and regularly skipping dinner (but not drinks). All was to no avail. At age 30 I was 30 pounds heavier than at age 20.

Criticism about my weight led to more than panic and crazy weight-loss schemes—it led to a loss of confidence. When I wasn't busy apologizing for being me, I was shopping, looking for that special item to bolster my self-esteem. Most of my clothes were too tight (dressing room mentality: the smaller the size, the less you weigh). A friend even commented in jest that I never let a size 10 tag interfere with my scooping up a "bargain."

A few years later, I read that a well-known U.S. senator's wife had worn a shocking see-through blouse to a staid Washington, D.C. reception. She later explained that at the time she was lacking in confidence and crying for attention. I thought immediately of all my attempts along the same line—of a certain silver lamé dress I had worn to an afternoon Harvard Club party and of those God-awful, sleazy, leatherette hot pants I had worn all over Boston—even to the Junior League. The latter outfit was particularly dazzling with the henna wig—circa 1972.

In my late twenties, I woke up one night in a cold sweat to the horrifying realization that I was never going

The night before my 30th birthday—and in a panic

to be thin, but that I was going to be 30. I wasn't sure which was worse. I had believed from childhood that acceptance and love were the rewards of youth, beauty and slimness. Youth and beauty were rapidly fading from the picture, and slimness seemed out of the question. I didn't know whether to cry or order a pizza.

My metamorphosis from fashion fool to fashion leader had an odd beginning. In the late 1970s I was manager of a Boston art gallery and had many wonderful friends and a sweet lifestyle. My dear friend Carol Nashe suggested that I go to Jordan Marsh department store and apply for a modeling job for a large-size catalog.

"Large-sized? Moi?" I asked doubtfully.

"Yes, you," she repeated.

Convinced, however, that the people at Jordan Marsh would laugh at a 32-year-old perfect size 14 (with perfect size 16 measurements), I spent a week compulsively polishing my nails and giving myself facials before venturing into possible Rejection-land. I had a week to do so only because the blizzard of 1978 closed down the city (and Jordan Marsh) for a week. In keeping with that theme, I was dressed all in winter white—like a giant snowflake—when I walked into Renee Bond's office in the store's advertising department.

Renee looked at me and said, "You're beautiful— you're just what I've been looking for!"

I literally looked over my shoulder to see if she might be speaking to someone else—so much for my confidence.

That "go see" (model audition) was the first of many successful ones that I would have. Renee became my friend and made it her pet project to make me more confident. Ironically, I soon found myself highly paid and a minor toast of the town for what had once been my fatal flaw—my size! One day a friend said, "Your picture is in the paper more than Jimmy Carter's." I was so tickled.

My dad had taught me that in life, one must learn to turn a lemon into lemonade. In my first year of modeling, I began to wear clothes that fit better and to be fanatical about my grooming. I learned to cast a

Modeling for Jordan Marsh (1979), where the fashion director said, "No more smiles! Go out there and show them dignity at a size 16!"

withering glance at anyone who made critical or hurtful remarks regarding weight—my weight or anybody else's. I must have been successful because one client said "You look so good, you make thin look boring!" I weighed 165 pounds and the world was applauding!

In 1979, my friend Beth Kramer, who owned a small part-time New York model agency called Big Beauties, decided to leave the city. She asked me if I would like to buy her business. I had no money, no desire to move to New York, and no experience running an agency, so of course I said "yes." I bought Big Beauties on July 24, 1979, with a $2,000 cash advance on my MasterCard, and began to commute weekly from Boston to New York.

Ad for Gloria Vanderbilt jeans. Good thing O's have relatively narrow hips!

Shooting on location in Florida. The O with a white belt—a big no-no!

On January 1, 1980, I moved lock, stock and current boyfriend from my beloved Beantown to the scary Big Apple (it's not so scary—it's wonderful), determined to be an overnight success. The agency consisted of an answering service, a few models Beth had found, and me. Today we are Big Beauties/Little Women, a

seven-figure corporation with close to 100 models.
Memories along the way are a blur of hard work,
personal slights ("Mary Who of Big What?"), raucous
laughter, good times, a major betrayal, bitter tears,
hard-learned lessons and wonderful, loyal friends,
workers and models.

Most of all, I remember a single, all-consuming
motivation. I was aware of what Carol Nashe, Renee
Bond and others had done for my shaky confidence. I
was sure that I could build my career and business while
doing the same for my models and for other women.

By the summer of 1981 I had become an experienced
fashion-show commentator. Having had no formal
training in fashion and clothing construction (although
my mother is a design whiz), I habitually read everything
I could find that pertained to style in general and to
large sizes in particular. One day, I read a magazine
article on the subject of female body shapes. I asked my
current boyfriend to describe my figure:

> ME: "Darling, how would you describe my
> figure?"
> HE: "Interesting." (So much for honesty.)
> ME: "What do you mean by 'interesting'?"
> HE: "You have no waist and your bust is bigger
> than your hips, which are rather squarish,
> but it's nice." (Last-minute attempt at tact.)
> ME: "Why do you love me if I'm such a lump?"
> HE: "I'll tell you someday."
> ME: "You'll do well to live that long."

Needless to say, I wasn't thrilled and began signing
notes to him from "The Waistless Wonder." I also began
to think about my specific shape—its good points and
limitations—and to look at my models and women I met
all across the country. Out of this process I developed
the **H-O-A-X** Formula.

The **H-O-A-X** Formula is more than a fashion gimmick
based on body shapes. It is a philosophy that enables
you to develop your own personal style through
self-evaluation, which in turn brings you greater
self-acceptance and happiness.

Developing a sense of personal style is a two-step process requiring a bit of self-analysis. The first step is to analyze:

- What counts in your life.
- What doesn't count.
- What you are willing or able to change.
- What you cannot change about yourself.

This analysis will take place in the rest of this chapter and in Chapter 8, *Defining Your Own Style.*

The second step and the subject of the remaining chapters in this book is to analyze:

- Your body shape.
- Your color preferences.
- Your lifestyle.
- Your personality.
- Your grooming.

WHAT COUNTS IN LIFE / WHAT DOESN'T

I believe that the most important parts of any human being are the *heart, soul* and *mind.* I further believe that the most wonderful traits a person can possess are *confidence, charm* and *style.*

There are so many reasons why confidence, charm and style are more important than flawless physical beauty—one of the best is that they age better. So do beauty of heart, soul and mind. Nevertheless, hardly a month goes by without an article in a major women's magazine about the beauty and fitness routines of one of the perennial super beauties: Joan Collins, Linda Evans, Linda Gray, Raquel Welch, Stephanie Powers, Elizabeth Taylor, Mitzi Gaynor, Debbie Reynolds, etc. We read, often with great admiration, of the disciplined regimens that keep these women young and beautiful. Often we feel inadequate and lazy after finishing such an article.

But why? What is so wonderful about spending 3 or 4 hours a day on your looks? Would you want a friend, daughter, mother or sister who was given to such extreme vanity? These super-beauties are celebrities whose livelihoods depend on their looks. Economic necessity mandates drastic action long after beauty naturally begins to fade.

Such is not the case for the *real* woman, nor in fact is it the case for great actresses. Think of Katharine Hepburn, Liv Ullman, Sada Thompson, Colleen Dewhurst, Claire Bloom, Helen Hayes and Shelley Winters. Have you ever read about their beauty routines? No! Nor have I ever read a word about the beauty regimes of Meryl Streep or Barbra Streisand, both of whom are super talents. These women are artists whose lives are too full to spend hours of time daily on unabashed shallowness and narcissism.

Extreme vanity is understandable when economic necessity is involved, but it is never admirable and rarely to be envied or emulated. A woman in the real world is too busy leading her life, developing her talents, working, and being friend, wife, mother, relative and good neighbor. She is the woman to whom I am speaking, the woman I admire—the woman with very little free time. She is the woman who wants to know how to look and feel her best, quickly and easily, which is what the H-O-A-X program is all about.

Statistically speaking, the average woman is 5′3.8″ tall, weighs 143 pounds, is 32.8 years old and wears a dress size 12 or 14. The important thing about this composite is that it shows the average woman is *not* the tall, extremely thin creature she has been led to believe she should be. Where do you fit in? More than likely you're average or above average in size, and of any age or height. More than likely you sometimes feel inadequate when confronted by a false media image of perfect womanhood.

Our feelings of inadequacy are created and exploited by industries dependent upon our financial support. Such industries (diet, exercise, cosmetic surgery, etc.) bombard us with the message: "Change, improve, you're never good enough." They manipulate us with breathtaking photos of the great beauties of the day, accompanied by copy designed to make us subtract points from ourselves until we gladly buy, buy, buy. So what if the ultimate price is a little more self-dissatisfaction?

We have become so self-critical that a recent magazine survey of 10,000 women concluded that 95% of us hate part or all of our bodies. This is a startling statistic! Many of us have turned against ourselves and toward the false promises of faddish and often dangerous or painful self-improvement schemes. Others have just given up.

FEAR OF FAT

This obsession with self-improvement has led to our new national pastime: dieting. It is the one activity for which most women seem to find time. This is even true for women who are not overweight when measured against standard height and weight charts.

In an ideal world, all women would:
- Eat three perfectly well-balanced meals a day totaling no more than 1800 calories.
- Exercise vigorously three times a week.
- Wear sensible shoes while walking 3 miles a day.
- Avoid alcohol and happy-hour munchies.
- Never wake up in the middle of the night dreaming of Hershey's or pepperoni.

In the real world, women:
- Sometimes eat 1800 calories for lunch alone.
- Think about exercise or start and stop exercise programs on a regular basis.
- Walk most vigorously from the TV to the refrigerator.
- Munch on snacks and drink cocktails before a big dinner.
- Think and talk about food even while eating.

Last year, Americans spent $11 billion on weight loss, yet only 3-5% of those who went on diets lost weight and kept it off. Diets are, for most of us, a failure experience that we regularly visit upon ourselves. They don't seem to work, in fact they may hurt. Diets can erode confidence, waste money, cause pain and guilt, and lower the metabolism. They train the chronic dieter to measure her worth by how few calories she can

When food and dieting become mutually exclusive obsessions
COURTESY SCHLOSSKY

consume—and to actually fear food. Contrary to sound H-O-A-X philosophy of "Make the most of what you've got," a dieter's philosophy is, "Be something else than what you are." Dieters walk the earth with a mindset of deprivation and are often miserable and resentful.

As a culture, we have a fear of fat, which we seem to define as anything *not* bone-thin. Further, while it is generally not acceptable to admit prejudice, prejudice against fat people seems to be acceptable. Many women of only moderate overweight, in fact, actually exhibit prejudice toward themselves. Such women are obsessed with diet and weight loss, yet remain frustrated in their efforts to gain "control" of their "problem." They yo-yo their weights and do severe psychological and physical damage to themselves—all for the Goddess of Thin. For such women, self-image and media image have become blurred on an unhappy merry-go-round.

Many women listen to diet doctors who say they cannot understand why any woman makes "the choice to be fat." This makes it sound as if it is a simple decision, the need for a little discipline rather than the undoing of a lifetime of eating habits, biological mandates and emotional reactions. They listen to people like me, who tell them that there is a particularly wide range of healthy weights for women. Then they look right to the lowest weight on the chart to plan their next daydream. They may even watch a TV report on the 20% of American college girls who are bulimic. And then what? The compulsive dieters go to their weight group meeting for their weekly weigh-in and pep-talk—and then go to lunch.

Dieting programs have a lower success rate than do the recovery programs for alcoholics and drug abusers. Dieting lowers self-esteem and reinforces negative body-imagery. To live to diet or to constantly try to change is a one-way trip down misery lane.

The average woman is a size 12-14, which means that 50% of us are above that median point. Weight-loss statistics seem to indicate that the vast majority of us are going to stay in that range. Isn't it better to accept that fact for the moment and to deal with reality?

The **H-O-A-X** diet credo is:

> *Whether you are 5 pounds or 105 pounds over what you think you should weigh, you're still the most gorgeous thing you've got.*

Get off weight as an excuse for what's wrong with your life, and get on to a positive track.

More and more of us are voicing our dissatisfaction with a media image of the "perfect woman"—tall, young, exquisite and ultra-thin.

Enough? I think so. For years I have been traveling the country telling women a simple, soothing, and truthful message: YOU HAVE THE POTENTIAL TO BE PERFECTLY SATISFIED WITH YOURSELF NO MATTER WHAT YOUR SIZE, AGE OR HEIGHT. You can get out of bed in the morning, embrace the new day and make the most of yourself as you really are. You can feel confident and oh so relieved to discover the joy of *not* dwelling on impossible self-improvement plans or on what is wrong with your appearance. Does that grab you? It's not impossible. I did it and you can too!

Before you let silly media images get you down, preventing you from finding the best of you, consider my partial list of the important things in life and add to it. Think about yourself and about the women you admire as you contemplate the following:

WHAT COUNTS	WHAT DOESN'T
Self-knowledge	Youth
Charm	Self-obsession
Confidence	Opinions of others
Style	Perfectionism
Heart	Material possessions
Soul	Fads
Mind	Exquisite natural beauty
Grooming	Miss America measurements
_____	_____
_____	_____
_____	_____

Most of what makes us happy comes from Column A. Most of what makes us unhappy—what we see as our shortcomings or flaws—comes from Column B. It's a half-full/half-empty-cup consideration. So begin to focus more on your positive potential.

While we're making lists, how about one on change? This is a partial change list for me. See how it works and make one for you.

WHAT I'D LIKE TO CHANGE AND HOW	POSSIBLE?	WILL I?	WHEN?
Lose weight	Yes	Probably not	???
Stop smoking	Yes	Yes	New Year's Day, 19??
Look 21	No	Get off it!!	
Work less, take more vacations	Yes	Yes	October
Socialize more	Yes	Maybe	When I retire or get rich, whichever comes first
Thick midriff	Yes	No—my body type	
Chubby back of neck/neck trouble	No	No—family trait	
___	___	___	___
___	___	___	___
___	___	___	___
___	___	___	___
___	___	___	___
___	___	___	___
___	___	___	___
___	___	___	___
___	___	___	___
___	___	___	___
___	___	___	___

Later in the book we will do more exercises and look at the best things about ourselves. You will want to refer back to this insightful inventory.

THE H-O-A-X FORMULA

This book is prescriptive—there are more how-to photographs, illustrations, charts, questionnaires and tips than there is heavy text. I believe that women want to *see* how to look their best. It is important to go through each chapter in order to find your best total look. I believe you will find this effort worthwhile, because the ultimate hoax is that none of us are naturally perfect. A woman's confidence comes from knowing that she has done the best with her physical self—and then getting on with her life.

Following is a breakdown of the book by chapters, with an explanation of what you can gain from each one.

Chapter 2
Which **H-O-A-X** *Body Type Are You?*

Many women cannot decide what body type they are, or think they are a combination of body types. It is important to choose *one* body type based on dominant features, selecting certain styles from what may be a secondary body type. For example, I am an **O** because of my midriff but have the high back hip and slightly more evenly proportioned thigh of the **H**. Therefore, I wear certain slightly fuller pants silhouettes of the **H** body, but in general, dress as an **O**.

Chapters 3-7
Dressing Your **H, O, A** *or* **X** *Body*

Each chapter is an overview of the best items of clothing for each figure shape. After reading the chapter for your body, you should review Chapter 7, *The* **H-O-A-X** *Glossary of Styles,* and make notes of new silhouettes you may wish to try.

Chapter 8
Defining Your Own Style

Personal style means knowing how to project your uniqueness to others. This chapter is extremely important, not only to fashion, but to self-knowledge and to feeling good about yourself.

Chapter 9
Shaping Your Body with Color, Texture and Line
Whether you have been color analyzed or not, this chapter shows you a fresh way to use color and all other things visual—texture, line and form—to "reshape" your body.

Chapter 10
Using Accessories the H-O-A-X *Way*
Add the crowning touches to your outfits and learn to draw attention to your best features through the proper use of accessories.

Chapters 11-12
Balancing Your Line with Great-Looking Hair and Makeup
The H-O-A-X process goes above the neck as balance, time, image and lifestyle are considered regarding hair and makeup. These chapters include unique questionnaires to find your best and most practical hair and makeup looks.

Chapter 13
Professional Grooming and Model Tips
This includes an easy system to make flawless grooming a natural, second-nature routine. Professional models have contributed their expertise with many tips and answers to your grooming questions.

Chapter 14
Planning and Organizing Your Wardrobe
A step-by-step guide to wardrobe and closet planning and maintenance is followed by tips on shopping, putting together a capsule wardrobe, and packing for travel.

Chapter 15
Golden Rules of the H-O-A-X *Formula*
I hope you will paste these feel-good rules to your mirror until you know them by heart. Now, let's go!

2

Which H-O-A-X *Body Type Are You?*

Knowing your measurements can make shopping easier.
COURTESY DON JACOBSON

AS I'VE SAID BEFORE, women's shapes fall into four distinct categories labeled with the letters H-O-A-X. The four shapes are universal, but that is *not* to say that all women of each shape are identical. Obviously women in each category provide many variations on a theme. Otherwise all H-shaped women would be clones, as would all O-, A- and X-shaped women—and we all know that each person is unique.

However, women in each H-O-A-X category have many body features in common. My goal is to show you how to identify your body type and recognize its characteristic features, and then teach you to accentuate or minimize whatever features you choose.

This chapter will help you decide what shape you have. First you will take your measurements. Based on these measurements, you will answer questions designed to pinpoint the sometimes subtle distinctions between one body type and another. You will also fill out a questionnaire analyzing the unique features of your body. These three steps should make clear whether you are an H, O, A or X, as well as identify specific characteristics you want to emphasize or de-emphasize.

Finally, we will discuss the garment industry's guidelines for sizing. Understanding sizing is essential in finding clothes that fit your body properly once you have determined whether you are an H, O, A or X.

HOW TO TAKE YOUR MEASUREMENTS

Accurate measurements are critical to determining your body type. Even if you already know your measurements, take them again and follow these instructions about where to measure:

1. **High Bust:** Under the arms and over the upper part of the breasts. This number is your correct bra size (i.e., 38-39 inches means you should wear a size 38 bra).
2. **Bust:** Across the back and over the nipples. Subtract this number from your high bust measurement. The difference tells you which of the following bra cup sizes you should wear:
   1 - 2 inches = A
   2 - 3 inches = B
   3 - 4 inches = C
   4 - 5 inches = D
   5 - 6 inches = DD
   6 - 8 inches = E
3. **Waist:** The narrowest part of the torso.
4. **High hip:** 3 inches down from the waist.
5. **Hip:** 7 inches down from the waist.
6. **Low hip** (both thighs together)**:** The widest part when both legs are together.
7. **Upper arm:** Under each armpit around the arm's fullest point.
8. **Thigh:** At the fullest part, around one thigh.
9. **Inseam:** Crotch to ankle bone.
10. **Front rise:** Crotch to waist.
11. **Hand:** First pinky knuckle to first thumb knuckle with hand closed.
12. **Back waist:** Nape of neck (visible bump when head bends forward) to waist.
13. **Sleeve:** Shoulder to wrist bone.

FINDING YOUR LETTER IN H-O-A-X

Answer the questions on the following pages for each body type. No matter how sure you are about your body

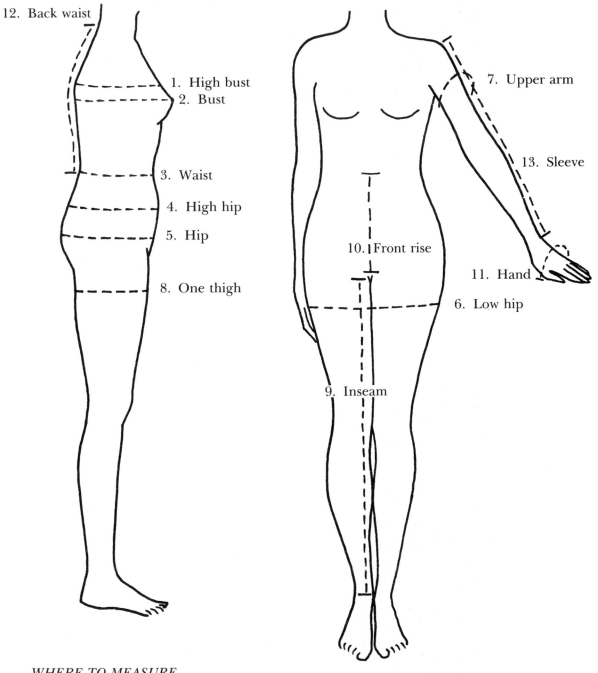

12. Back waist

1. High bust
2. Bust

3. Waist

4. High hip

5. Hip

8. One thigh

7. Upper arm

13. Sleeve

10. Front rise

11. Hand

6. Low hip

9. Inseam

WHERE TO MEASURE

type, answer all four sets of questions. Then count your "yes" answers for each body type. The letter for which you have the most "yes" answers is your body shape. Even if two scores are equal or very close, you are still

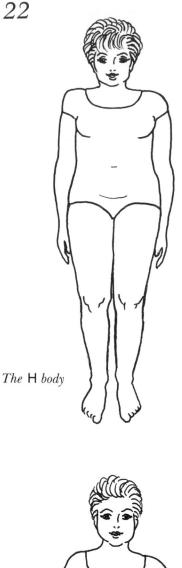

The H body

one dominant body type with *some* traits of another. To decide which of the body types is dominant, answer the additional questions on pages 24 and 25. Bear in mind that many women have a trait or two that is atypical for their body type.

H

Is the difference between your bust and hip (#2 and #5) less than 2 inches?

Is the difference between the smaller of these two measurements (bust and hip) and your waist no more than 8 inches?

Does your hip area have a squarish appearance, with your high hip (#4) measuring closer to your hip (#5) than to your waist?

Is your back or neck fleshy?

Is your face or neck full in proportion to the rest of your profile?

Are your arms and legs slim in proportion to the rest of your body?

O

Is your hip (#5) no more than 1 inch larger (or actually smaller) than your bust?

Does your figure appear larger above the waist than below?

Is your lower hip (#6) noticeably smaller than your high hip and hip (#4 and #5)?

Stand naturally in profile without pulling in your middle. Is your bust, midriff or tummy protuberant?

Is there a collection of fat at the back of your neck (dowager's hump)?

Are your legs particularly slim and shapely in proportion to your torso?

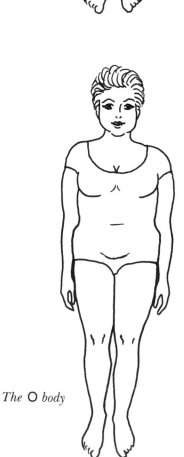

The O body

A

Is the difference between your bust and hip (#2 and #5) 2 inches or more?

Is your waist clearly defined and at least 9 inches smaller than the smaller of these two (bust and hip) measurements?

Is your hip rounded or curvy?

Is your lower hip (#6) as big as or bigger than your hip measurement (#5)?

Is your face slim in proportion to your overall body proportion?

Do your bust and shoulder line appear small or moderate in proportion to the rest of your body?

Are your legs average-sized or large?

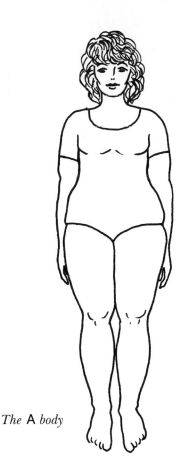

The **A** *body*

X

Is your hip (#5) the same or no more than 2 inches larger than your bust (#2)? (If your bust is bigger than your hip, you are an **O**.)

Is your waist at least 9 inches smaller than the smaller of these (bust and hip)?

Do your upper arms tend to be full in proportion to the rest of your body?

From profile, does your waist definitely curve inward?

Does your torso have an hourglass shape?

Are your legs slim or average and your thighs curvy or fleshy?

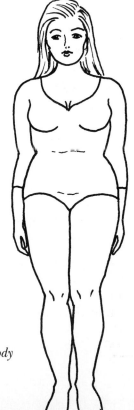

The **X** *body*

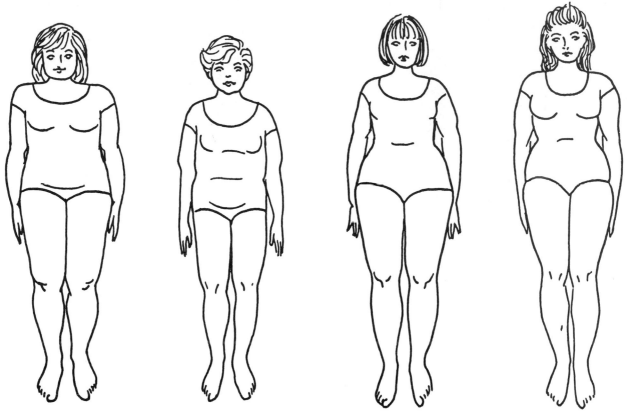

Shorter, wider **H-O-A-X** *figures*

IF YOU CAN'T DECIDE

If you are torn between two body types, consider the following points. Bear in mind that many women have a trait or two that is atypical of their predominant body type (i.e., an **A** with a midriff bulge or an **H** with large thighs). In such a case, you must use common sense in choosing clothes that do not cling, draw horizontal lines or otherwise exaggerate or draw attention to these subtraits.

If you can't decide between:

- An **H** and an **O**—Are you straight up and down from the front view (**H**) or do your thighs appear narrower than your high hip (**O**)?
- An **H** and an **A**—Is your hip/thigh area square in appearance from front view (**H**) or is it very full, becoming fullest at the lower hip/thigh area (**A**)?

H-O-A-X *in sizes 14 and 16*

- An **H** and an **X**—Is your waist indented from your rib cage (**X**) or are your rib cage and waist straight (**H**)?
- An **O** and an **A**—Is your hip measurement (#5) the same or smaller than your bust (**O**) or larger (**A**)?
- An **O** and an **X**—Are your hips as full and round as your bust (**X**) or are they noticeably smaller and straighter in form (**O**)?
- An **A** and an **X**—Is your hip or lower hip (whichever is wider) at least 2 inches bigger than your bust (**A**), or do you not have much lower hip/thigh bulge and are all your hip measurements well-proportioned to your bust?

Once you have determined your body type and finished reading this chapter, proceed to the chapter for your body type (Chapter 3, 4, 5 or 6), and then to the style glossary in Chapter 7 to see illustrations of your best styles.

PERSONAL FIGURE ANALYSIS

PART 1: EVALUATING YOUR BODY

Very few women have the fashion world's ideal figure, much less the doctor's-chart ideal weight. Once you have taken your measurements, stand in your bra and panties before a full-length mirror and give your body an honest evaluation. Circle all of the following that apply to you:

Overall Size:	Small, average, large, extra-large
Height:	Short, medium, tall
Head (including hair):	Small, medium, large
Jaw:	Firm, soft, full, weak, prominent, flabby
Neck:	Short, average, long, thin, medium, wide, angular
Shoulders:	Broad, average, narrow, sloped, rounded, angular
Back:	Straight, curved, fleshy, wide, average, narrow
Bust:	Small, average, prominent
Arms:	Fleshy, average, thin, smooth, lumpy, hairy
Hands:	Large, average, small, rough, smooth
Fingers:	Long, short, thin, fleshy, average
Midriff:	Flat, average, prominent
Waist:	Small, average, large, high, low, missing in action
Tummy:	Flat, curved, full
High Hip:	Full, curved, flat
Lower Hip:	Round, square, pear, figure 8
Derriere:	Flat, curved, prominent
Thighs:	Small, average, large, lumpy, smooth
Knees:	Bony, fleshy, dimpled, average
Calves:	Slim, average, large, fleshy, curvy
Ankles:	Small, average, large, fleshy
Feet:	Small, average, large, narrow, medium width, wide

PART 2: ANALYZING YOUR FIGURE FEATURES

Referring to Part 1, list below the parts of your body that you particularly like and those that you find particularly problematic. As you proceed through the chapters to follow, you will learn to de-emphasize what some might call *figure problems*, regarding them instead as *figure features*. More importantly, you will learn to emphasize your favorite figure features, focusing on the positive.

	I Wish to Emphasize	*I Wish to De-emphasize*
Height	_____	_____
Head	_____	_____
Face	_____	_____
Jaw	_____	_____
Neck	_____	_____
Shoulders	_____	_____
Back	_____	_____
Bust	_____	_____
Arms	_____	_____
Hands	_____	_____
Fingers	_____	_____
Midriff	_____	_____
Tummy	_____	_____
High Hip	_____	_____
Hip	_____	_____
Derriere	_____	_____
Thighs	_____	_____
Knees	_____	_____
Calves	_____	_____
Ankles	_____	_____
Feet	_____	_____

UNDERSTANDING SIZING

For years we have measured dozens of women (prospective models) each week who have answered the agency's open call. We never cease to be amazed by the number of women who list their dress size as the smallest-sized garment they have ever owned.

Manufacturer sizing charts vary tremendously (my latest wardrobe runs from sizes 12 to 20, and I am a 16), but every woman should know her size in terms of standard sizing. You may not like the numbers, but it is best to be realistic.

Since the 1960s, manufacturers have made their clothes larger and larger. Today's size 10 was a 12 or 14 in 1965. (In 1950, a woman who wore size 2 or 4 was probably deathly ill—or worse!) The reason manufacturers have made clothing larger is to flatter our vanity. However, this flattery backfires when we try on a garment and decide whether or not to buy it based on its size tag rather than on how it fits.

Therefore, chart your measurements for height, bust, waist and hip, and determine your correct size and size categories. Then realize that you may actually own clothes two sizes *larger* or *smaller* but that *the number of the size tag does not make you fatter or thinner.*

Following are standard size specifications. All measurements are variable up to 2 inches, as they are an average of many sizing charts.

JUNIOR

Description:
- 5′2″ to 5′7″ in height
- Short- or average-waisted, with waist proportionally fuller than Missy
- Bust somewhat smaller and higher than Missy
- Generally a youngish body, but can be any age
- Juniors are sized 3-15

JUNIOR SIZE CHART							
SIZE	3	5	7	9	11	13	15
BUST	32	33	34	35.5	37	38	40
WAIST	24	25	26	27.5	29	30	31
HIP	34	35	36	37.5	39	40	41

MISSY

Description:
- 5′4″ to 5′7″ in height
- Normal or long-waisted
- Womanly proportions
- Missy is sized 4-20

MISSY SIZE CHART

SIZE	4	6	8	10	12	14	16	18	20
BUST	33	34	35	36	38	39	40	42	44
WAIST	23	24	25	26	28	29	30	32	34
HIPS	33	34	35	36	38	40	42	43	45

PETITE

Description:
- 5′4″ and under in height
- Medium or delicate shoulder
- Average or short waist
- Any age, delicate body
- Petite is sized 2P to 16P

PETITE SIZE CHART

SIZE	2P	4P	6P	8P	10P	12P	14P	16P
BUST	32	33	34	35	36	38	39	41
WAIST	22	23	24	25	26	28	29	31
HIPS	33	34	35	36	37	38	40	41.5

WOMEN'S

Description:
- Medium or wide shoulders
- Waist proportionally larger than Missy
- Hips somewhat fuller than bust
- Women's sizes are 14W to 26W

Note—As of 1986, Women's sizes have changed.
Women's old sizes ranged from 34 to 46 for tops and 28

to 40 for bottoms. A comparison of new and old sizes appears below.

WOMEN'S SIZE CHART

OLD TOP SIZE	34	36	38	40	42	44	46
OLD BOTTOM SIZE	28	30	32	34	36	38	40
NEW SIZE	14W	16W	18W	20W	22W	24W	26W
BUST	39	41	43	45	47	49	51
WAIST	30	32	34	36	38	40	42
HIPS	40	42	44	46	48	50	52

HALF SIZES

Description:
- 5′1″ to 5′6″
- Full bust
- Short waist
- Full tummy
- Narrow or average shoulder

Note—As of 1986, Half Sizes have changed to Women's Petite (WP) sizes. Old half sizes ranged from 12½ to 26½. A comparison of new and old sizes appears below.

HALF SIZE (WOMEN'S PETITE) CHART

OLD HALF SIZE	12½	14½	16½	18½	20½	22½	24½	26½
NEW WP SIZE	12WP	14WP	16WP	18WP	20WP	22WP	24WP	26WP
BUST	37	39	41	43	45	47	49	51
WAIST	29	31	33	35	37	39	41	43
HIPS	38	40	42	44	46	48	50	52

*LINGERIE**

P	S	M	L	1X	2X	3X	4X
4	6-8	10-12	14-16	16-18	20-22	24	26

*These sizes are also used for T-shirts, sweaters, knits, etc.

MY SIZES

Bra (see page 20)   _____

Lingerie   _____

Clothes   Category

       *_____   _____

       *_____   _____

       *_____   _____

*Give or take two (2) sizes (whether a given garment is *larger* or *smaller* than the size you usually wear makes no difference). You should never wear clothes that are snug!

SIGN, FINGERPRINT, NOTARIZE, PLEDGE, & INITIAL

_____

3

The H Figure

"Anyplace I hang my pantyhose is my waist."
—MARY PAT, DALLAS, TEXAS, 1986

DESCRIPTION: THE STRAIGHT UP-AND-DOWN FIGURE

Goal: To de-emphasize the lack of a waist or to create the illusion of a smaller or more indented midsection.

DETAILS

The H body type has the following features:

Face: Usually square, rectangular, round or full-jawed oval.

Neck: Usually short with a tendency toward fullness at the nape (dowager's hump—who thought up that name?)

Bust: Usually small or medium, although weight or childbirth may bring additional fullness.

Back: Usually broad with a tendency to gain weight above and below the bra line.

Waist: Not clearly defined, with a tendency toward a puffy midriff and side or back love handles. If your waist is 10 inches smaller than your bust or hips, you *are not* an H.

Thighs: Rarely bigger than the high hip, and usually a bit smaller. Exaggerated thigh bulge is *almost never* an H problem.

Legs and Arms: Usually slim or average in proportion to overall body weight. The H is torso-heavy with more delicate limbs. Upper arms and thighs may have some cellulite.

Best Features: Hips, thighs, arms, bust and legs. The H figure looks best in flowing, graceful styles. High-fashion models are usually H types. Average and large

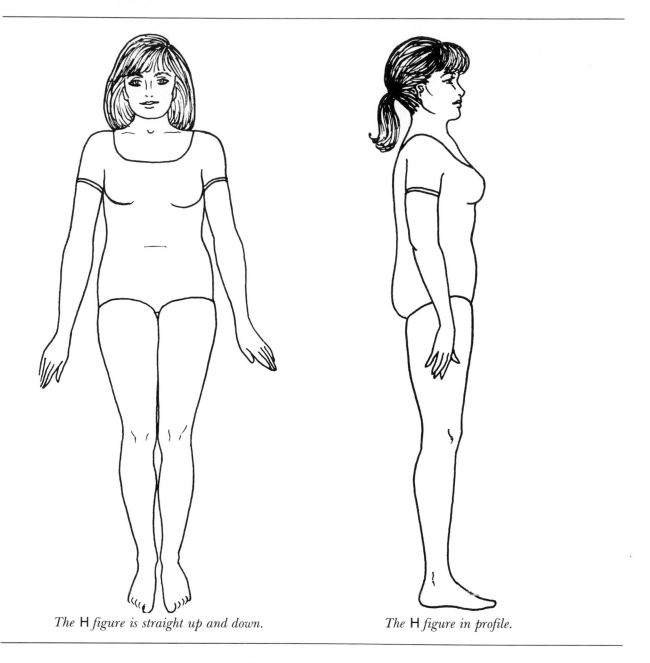

The H *figure is straight up and down.*

The H *figure in profile.*

H's should learn to project a body image that is *proportioned,* not *straight.* Many fashion designers consider the H figure the easiest shape to dress.

Worst Features: Straight waist; high hip; tendency toward lumpiness in the middle and upper back; short neck with full nape; tendency to develop a protruding stomach; negative self-image caused by lack of feminine curves.

Like so many H *women, Deborah looks best in soft dressing (left). The structured career-look blazer makes her look wider and less graceful.*

℞ FOR DRESSING THE H

The most flattering lines for an H accomplish the following (an example is included for each point):

- Create the illusion of a smaller midsection (elasticized belts).
- Distract from the middle torso (hip wraps).
- Emphasize thighs, lower hips and legs (long, banded sweaters).
- Cover or slim the back of the neck (portrait necklines).
- Elongate with vertical lines (coat dresses, plackets, long pearls and V-necks).
- De-emphasize a heavy back (loose sweaters, body briefers, camisoles).

The H should look for styles that draw the eye *out* at shoulder, hip and thigh and *in* at the midsection. The H should also look for lines that are long, graceful, vertical and fluid. All styles listed below as do's and don'ts for the **H** are illustrated in Chapter 7, *The* **H-O-A-X** *Glossary of Styles*.

THE BEST STYLES FOR H BODIES

DRESSES: THE BEST

2-piece shirtdress	Flapper	Shirtwaist chemise
Elastic waist	Blouson	Coat dress
V-yoke	Fanny wrap	Jumper
Peasant	Tie front	Slip dress
2-piece blouson	Float	Tabard
Tunic dress	Bib dress	Sweater dress
2-piece overblouse	Muu-muu	A-line
Bubble	Sheath	Empire
Drop waists to the hip or thigh	Princess	Cocoon
	Chemise	Thigh wrap

The asymmetric fanny-wrap dress works on the **H** *body (left), but not on the* **O**, *whose bust and midriff are more prominent.*

Audrey's overalls are fun, young and slim over the H waist.

Cropped pants and top with a long cardigan jacket and dramatic hat give H Jeannie a cool, sleek, natural-fiber look.

COURTESY ROYAL WOMAN

PANTS: THE BEST

Straight leg	Short culotte	Wide-leg cuffed
Peg leg	Culotte	short
Stirrup	Clam digger	Tap pant
Legging	Pull-on	Boxer shorts
Cropped	Pleated trouser	Jamaicas
Capri	Jumpsuit	Bermudas
Knicker	Overall	Walking short
Toreador	Short-short	Wide-leg walking
Pedal pusher	Shorts	short
Hip yoke		Skort

SKIRTS: THE BEST

Straight	A-line	Golf
Pegged/Hobble	Jean skirt	Knife pleat
Inverted pleat	Side slit	Crystal pleat
Kick pleat	Slit	Gored
Wrap	Modified dirndl	Border print
Inset pleat	Tube	Hip yoke
Godet	Gaucho	Handkerchief
Trumpet	Split	Side pleat

TOPS: THE BEST

Bow	Sailor	Shell
Poet/Victorian	Hip-yoke blouson	Skimp
Peasant	Sport	Cowl
Blouson	Button-down	Tunic
Notched/	Camp	Sweater vest
Convertible	Collarband	Tank
collar	Cardigan	Camisole
Collarless front	V-neck cardigan	Sweatshirt
button	Pullover	Overblouse
Fanny wrap	Crew	T-shirt

The drop-blouson top and long trumpet skirt on Greta are among the best looks for both H *and* O *women.*
COURTESY JEFF FLAX

Broad shoulders and curved lines at the side create the illusion of a waist for the H.
COURTESY JUDITH & CO.

COATS: THE BEST

Cape	Trench	Polo
Sherlock Holmes cape	Chesterfield	Reefer
	Quilted	Slicker
Smock	Shawl	Fling
Fitted	Wrap	Duster

JACKETS: THE BEST

Parka	Mao	Tuxedo
Pea	Nehru	Norfolk
Topper	Blazer	Safari
Car coat	Eton	Fly-away
Stroller	Spencer	Semifitted
Battle jacket		

VESTS: THE BEST

Sweater vest	Tabard	Maude

COLLARS & NECKLINES: THE BEST

Convertible	Batteau	Chelsea
Button-down	V-neck	Shawl
Johnny	Sweetheart	Portrait
Collarband	Décolleté	Sailor
Crew	Keyhole	Cowl
Jewel	Camisole	Grecian
Drawstring	Asymmetric	Tuxedo
Jabot	Notched	Peter Pan
Bow		

SLEEVES: THE BEST

Short	Angel	Raglan (padded)
Cap	Dolman	Long-fitted
Drop	Batwing	Seven-eighths
Bell	Poet	Minimal
Tulip	Ruffled	Shirtsleeve
Flutter	Pleated puff	French cuff
Cape		

LINGERIE / FOUNDATIONS & DAYWEAR: THE BEST

Body briefer	Longline strapless	Full slip
Merry widow	bra	Tap pant
Waist cincher	Sport bra	Camisole
Control brief	Contour bra	Brief
Corselette	Convertible-strap	Split petticoat
Soft-cup bra	bra	Shoulder pad
Underwire bra	Push-up bra	Teddy
Longline bra	Half slip	

LINGERIE / AT-HOME & SLEEPWEAR: THE BEST

Baby doll	Empire gown	Hostess coat
Shorty pajama	Granny gown	Robe (unbelted)
Sleepshirt	Caftan	Kimono
Oversize T-shirt	Illusion caftan	Peignoir and
Pajama	Housecoat	negligee

SWIMWEAR: THE BEST

Maillot	Tank	Gathered
Strapless	Halter	French cut
Boy leg	V-neck	Strapless maillot
Blouson	Sarong	

Don't: The bulky sweater widens the H upper torso, and sneakers make her legs unattractive.

WHAT THE H SHOULD AVOID

In general, the H should avoid any garment that emphasizes the straight, boxy quality of the waistline, minimizes the shoulder and hip lines, or has a boxy, square, wide shape.

THE WORST STYLES FOR H BODIES

SKIRTS: THE WORST

Hipster	Flared/Semicircle	Bubble
Box pleat	Gathered	Bell
Kilt	Circle	Tiered
High waist	Peasant	

Don't: Horizontal lines at the H *upper torso create a bulky, boxy look.*

Do: An elastic waist in a soft fabric dress creates the illusion of a more-defined middle for the H.

DRESSES: THE WORST

Set-in waist sheath	Schoolgirl blouson	Longuette/Bustier
Set-in waist dirndl	Pinafore	Drop waist (slight)
Cinch waist	Prairie	Baby-doll smock
Surplice	Square dance	Tent
Wrap	Sundress	1-piece shirtdress
Peplum	Strapless	

PANTS: THE WORST

Jean	Harem	Wide-leg walking
Bell bottom	Jodhpur	short
Palazzo	Wide-leg Bermuda	Romper

Padded shoulders, long jackets or tunics, monochromatic dressing and soft layers soften the squarish lines of the H body.

Jeannie's blouson leotard is a good bet for the H or O figure, but how does she kick so high?

TOPS: THE WORST

Ruffled front	Polo	Turtleneck
Cossack	Lumberjack	Fisherman
Surplice	Poor boy	Halter

COATS, JACKETS & VESTS: THE WORST

Swagger coat	Redingote	Waist coat
Balmacan	Peplum coat	Bolero vest
Princess coat	Bolero coat	Wing-back jacket

COLLARS & NECKLINES: THE WORST

Winged	Cossack	Halter vee
Bermuda	Bib	Square
Turtle	Pierrot	Drape
Halter	Victorian	Off-shoulder
Nehru	Ruffle	Strapless
Mandarin	Scoop	Teardrop
Bertha		

SLEEVES: THE WORST

Sleeveless	Halter	Three-quarter
Baby doll	Bishop	fitted
Puff	Gibson	Elbow
Carmen Miranda		

LINGERIE: THE WORST

Panty girdle	Strapless bra	T-shirt
Thigh panty girdle	Bikini panties	Waist-tie bathrobe
Capri girdle	Hipster panties	Petticoat
Boned girdle		

SWIMSUITS: THE WORST

2-piece	Dressmaker	Set-in skirt
Bikini	Jewel neck	Surplice

Longer jackets with hose and shoes coordinated to the color of the hem give H *Liz a long, fluid, lean look.*

SPECIAL NOTES FROM A SPECIAL H

Model and motivational speaker Liz Dillon is a very chic H. Here are some of her best looks:

- Shoulder pads
- Extended (dropped) or dolman sleeves
- Belts with important buckles or sashes dropped gently below the waist
- Long jackets, tunics or vests over long skirts
- Man-tailored shirt collars turned up
- Matching skirts, hose and shoes
- Body briefers instead of bras and girdles
- Man-tailored slouchy or oversized looks à la Dietrich
- Dramatic flourishes that distract the eye from a non-existent waist:
    - Layers
    - Paisley shawls over one shoulder
    - Hats, head wraps
    - Large-scale jewelry
    - Fabrics that shine or move gracefully

Liz's best tip is: "Good posture!"

4

The O Figure

"I'm an egg with legs."
—VIRGINIA, NEW YORK CITY, 1984

DESCRIPTION: THE ROUND- OR OVAL-TORSO FIGURE

Goal: To de-emphasize the prominent front body section (bust, tummy or midriff) and the lack of a waist, emphasizing legs that are often lovely. A second goal is to create the illusion of length and better balance between the full torso and slimmer legs and thighs.

DETAILS

The O body type has the following features:

Face: Usually square, round or pear-shaped with a fleshy jaw and cheek area. The O face is usually large or full in relation to overall body size.

Neck: Short with a tendency toward fullness at the nape of the neck and shoulders.

Bust: Medium or large. The O bust will usually measure more than the hips, causing the O woman to think she is a V. (But then this book would be called H-A-V-O-X!)

Back: Broad with a tendency toward fleshiness, especially above the bra.

Waist: Not clearly defined. The O waist disappears totally with weight gain. Unlike her H sister, the O woman frequently feels that her waistline girth is in front more than at the side. Midriff bulge is the O's trademark.

Hips: Usually flat in the rear and much smaller in the thigh than in the high hip. From bust to ankle, the O feels like a triangle.

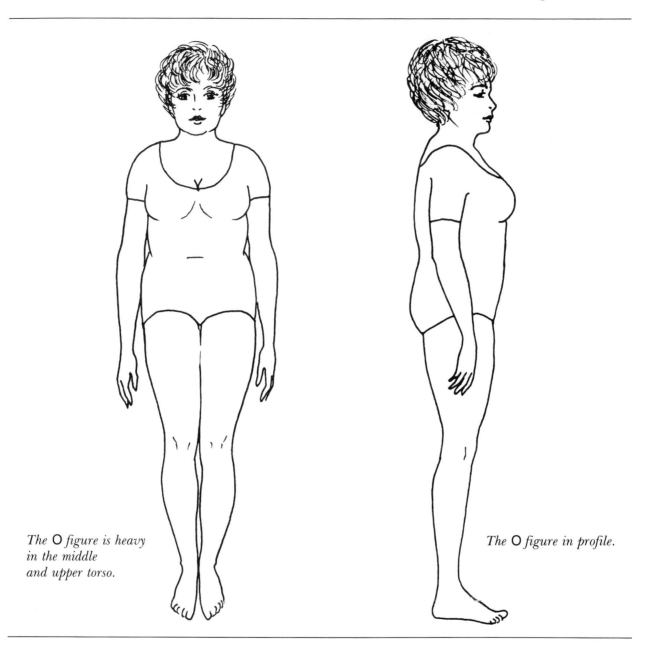

The O *figure is heavy in the middle and upper torso.*

The O *figure in profile.*

Thighs: Slim and shapely with possible fullness at the high thigh only. The thighs are the narrowest point of the O torso.

Legs and Arms: Usually slender in proportion to the body, especially the lower legs and lower arms. Slender legs can make her look top heavy, but properly emphasized, legs can be her greatest asset.

*The "Austrian Shade" cocktail dress is a disaster on **A** Susan (left) and superb on **O** Gail, who are both a size 22. An **O** emphasizes her hip and thigh area while an **A** doesn't.*

Best Features: Hips, thighs, legs and arms. The **O** has a figure that is usually short or average in height and looks best when she wears styles that draw the eye away from the torso and toward the thighs, legs and face. She is often told by friends, "You look adorable" when she thinks she looks sophisticated.

Worst Features: Neck, nape of neck, chin, high back, waist and either midriff, bust or tummy. The **O** woman fears that she looks like a beach ball on stilts and longs to get away from the "cuteness" of many of her best looks.

℞ FOR DRESSING THE O

The most flattering lines for an **O** accomplish the following (an example is included for each point):

- Make the waist appear indented (elasticized belt with blousoned V-neck shirt).
- Distract from the middle torso (hip-banded blouson).

This dress (left) couldn't be worse for an O*: set-in waist, sash with rosette, two-tones cutting her in half, and hiking at the back hip. Vertical stripes on top, however, elongate and narrow Gail's torso.*

Rita, an O*, in a dress (left) with stripes going in the wrong direction on the upper torso, and in one of her best silhouettes, a floral drop-waist blouson.*

- Draw the eye to the thighs and legs (stirrup pants and tunic sweater).
- De-emphasize a heavy back (non-clingy fabrics, body briefers, camisoles or full slips).
- Create the illusion of height, length and grace (long pearls, monotone outfits).

The **O** should look for garments that de-emphasize the torso. Styles should (1) be balanced by an emphatic shoulder and the illusion of a wider hipline, or (2) have an exaggerated wedge-shape that follows the body's line from shoulder to narrow hip. The **O** has the fewest silhouettes of any shape and may be the hardest body to dress, but there is *plenty* from which to choose. Only the **O** has the dual options of exaggerating her wedge (**V**) shape or of balancing it.

All styles listed below as do's and don'ts for the **O** are illustrated in Chapter 7, *The* **H-O-A-X** *Glossary of Styles*.

Do: A uniform among O's is the oversized sweater with shoulder pads over slim leggings. This look exaggerates her natural wedge shape.

THE BEST STYLES FOR O BODIES

DRESSES: THE BEST

2-piece shirtdress (elastic waist)	Flapper	Muu-muu
2-piece blouson	Blouson	Chemise (soft fabric)
Tunic dress	Drop blouson	Shirtwaist chemise (soft fabric)
Bubble	Fanny wrap	
2-piece overblouse	Thigh wrap	Jumper
Drop waist (to hip or thigh)	Tie front	Tabard
Drop waist (elastic)	Cocoon	Sweater dress
	Float	
	Bib dress	

PANTS: THE BEST

Peg leg	Hip yoke	Tap pant
Stirrup	Overall	Boxer short
Legging	Short short	Skort (elastic waist)
Cropped	Shorts	Bermudas
Capri	Wide-leg, cuffed short (elastic waist)	Jamaicas
Toreador		Pull-on elastic waist
Pedal pusher		

"Curvy and over 40" (as O Kathleen calls herself) is elegant and dressed in proportion to her height and shape in a two-piece overblouse dress.

SKIRTS: THE BEST

Straight	Trumpet (elastic waist)	Gaucho
Pegged/Hobble	Side slit (elastic waist)	Golf
Inverted pleat		Crystal pleat
Kick pleat	Slit (elastic waist)	Border print
Inset pleat	Modified dirndl	Hip yoke (elastic waist)
Godet (elastic waist)	Tube	

TOPS: THE BEST

Ruffled front	Fanny wrap	V-neck cardigan
Blouson	Sailor	Skimp
Notched/ Convertible collar	Hip-yoke blouson	Cowl
	Sport	Tunic
	Button-down	Sweatshirt
Collarless button front	Cardigan	Overblouse

COATS, JACKETS & VESTS: THE BEST

Cape	Slicker	Stroller
Sherlock Holmes cape	Duster	Parka
	Pea jacket	Battle jacket
Smock	Topper	Mao jacket
Fling	Car coat	Wing-back jacket
Chesterfield	Fly-away jacket	Tabard vest
Polo/Overcoat	Semifitted jacket	Maude vest

COLLARS & NECKLINES: THE BEST

Convertible	Décolleté	Portrait
Button-down	Notched	Sailor
Peter Pan	Chelsea	Cowl
Crew	Shawl	Tuxedo
V-neck		

SLEEVES: THE BEST

Sleeveless	Bell	Ruffled
Cap	Angel	Long fitted
Drop	Dolman	Seven-eighths
Flutter	Batwing	Shirtsleeve
Cape	Poet	French cuff
Tulip		

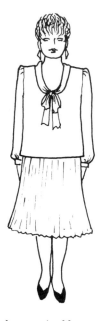

Do: The drop-waist blouson with crystal pleats creates a look that balances the O *figure by making the bottom lines a bit fuller.*

LINGERIE / FOUNDATIONS & DAYWEAR: THE BEST

Body briefer	Longline bra	Camisole
Merry widow	Longline strapless	Teddy
Waist cincher	bra	Brief
Control brief	Full slip	Tap pant
Corselette	Half slip	Shoulder pad
Underwire bra	Split petticoat	

LINGERIE / AT HOME & SLEEPWEAR: THE BEST

Baby doll	Granny gown	Housecoat
Shorty pajama	Caftan	Robe (unbelted)
Sleepshirt	Illusion caftan	Peignoir and
Oversize T-shirt	Hostess coat	negligee

SWIMWEAR: THE BEST

Maillot	French cut	Sarong
Boy leg	Tank	Gathered
Blouson	V-neck	Strapless maillot

WHAT THE O SHOULD AVOID

The O should avoid garments that (1) bring the eye to the fullest part of the center torso, or (2) draw the eye in at the shoulder or shoulder-and-thigh areas.

THE WORST STYLES FOR O BODIES

DRESSES: THE WORST

Set-in waist sheath	Pinafore	Empire
Set-in waist dirndl	Prairie	Baby-doll smock
1-piece shirtdress	Square dance	Tent
Elastic waist	Sundress	Sheath
Cinch waist	Strapless	Princess
Surplice	Longuette/Bustier	Coat dress
Wrap	V-yoke	Slip dress
Peplum	Peasant	A-line
Schoolgirl blouson	Drop waist (slight)	

Don't: The raglan-sleeve bulky sweater tucked into wide pleated trousers defines the O's waist.

PANTS: THE WORST

Straight leg*	Pleated trousers	Walking short
Jean	Bell	Wide-leg Bermuda
Knicker	Palazzo	Wide-leg walking
Short culotte	Harem	short
Culotte	Jodhpur	Romper
Clam digger	Jumpsuit	

*For most O figures, the straight leg will be too full in the thigh if it fits properly in the waist. With alterations (letting waist out and/or taking thigh in), this silhouette will work.

SKIRTS: THE WORST

Wrap	Knife pleat	Circle
Side pleat	Kilt	Peasant
A-line	Gored	Bubble
Jean skirt	High waist	Bell
Split	Flared/Semicircle	Tiered
Hipster	Gathered	Handkerchief
Box pleat		

TOPS: THE WORST

Bow	Lumberjack	Sweater vest*
Poet/Victorian	Collarband*	Fisherman
Cossack	Pullover	Tank
Surplice	Crew	Halter
Peasant	Shell	Camisole
Polo	Poor boy	T-shirt
Camp*	Turtleneck	

*Can work when worn as a jacket, unbuttoned.

COATS, JACKETS & VESTS: THE WORST

Swagger coat	Wrap	Safari jacket
Balmacan	Reefer	Peplum jacket
Fitted coat	Blazer	Bolero jacket
Princess	Eton jacket	Nehru jacket
Trench	Spencer jacket	Sweater vest
Redingote	Tuxedo jacket	Waist coat
Quilted coat	Norfolk jacket	Bolero vest
Shawl		

50

The O uniform again: Narrow pants emphasizing a slim leg, and an oversized sweater with padded shoulders.

COLLARS & NECKLINES: THE WORST

Johnny	Pierrot	Sweetheart
Winged	Bib	Halter Vee
Bermuda	Ruffle	Keyhole
Collarband	Victorian	Camisole
Jewel	Drawstring	Asymmetric
Halter	Jabot	Off-shoulder
Turtle	Bow	Scoop
Mandarin	Batteau	Drape
Nehru	Teardrop	Grecian
Cossack	Square	Strapless
Bertha		

SLEEVES: THE WORST

Short	Halter	Raglan
Baby doll	Bishop	Three-quarters
Puff	Pleated puff	Elbow
Carmen Miranda	Gibson	Minimal

LINGERIE / FOUNDATIONS & DAYWEAR: THE WORST

Panty girdle	Strapless bra	Petticoat
Thigh panty girdle	Contour bra	Bikini panty
Capri girdle	Sport bra	T-shirt
Boned girdle	Push-up bra	Hipster
Soft-cup bra	Convertible bra	

LINGERIE / AT HOME & SLEEPWEAR: THE WORST

Pajama	Bathrobe	Kimono

SWIMWEAR: THE WORST

2-piece	Strapless	Jewel neck
Bikini	Dressmaker	Set-in skirt
Surplice	Halter	

Lyne, an O, *in a slim leather skirt and oversized blouse tied at the hip, puts all the emphasis on her great legs.*
COURTESY RUGEN KOREY

SPECIAL NOTES FROM A SPECIAL O

Model Lyne Pedola is a beautiful O. These are some of her best styles and accessories:

- Oversized sweaters that end at the thigh
- Leggings and stirrup pants
- Tunics
- Simple, collarless suit jackets
- Full-length leather skirts
- 1-1/2-inch heels instead of flats
- Shoes with an open vamp
- Scarves in hair
- Short boots
- Shoulder pads
- Skimps
- Big jewelry
- Soft chemises that narrow at the hem so as not to fall off the bust like a shelf
- Flared shorts
- Vertical lines such as beads or scarves
- Underwire bras or minimizer bras
- No big ruffles, decorative buttons or fussy tops

The A Figure

DESCRIPTION: THE HIP- OR THIGH-HEAVY FIGURE

Goal: To de-emphasize the heaviness below the waist, to emphasize the well-defined waist, and to create a better sense of balance between the upper and lower torso.

DETAILS

The **A** body type has the following features:

Face: Usually oval, rectangular, heart or pear-shaped with a nicely defined, rather firm chin. The **A** face tends to be thin in relation to overall body size.

Neck: Slender and average or long in length. The **A** rarely has a "dowager's hump" at the nape of the neck or chubbiness in the neck and shoulder area. Instead, shoulders are medium or narrow on most **A** bodies. Many **A**'s complain of crepiness in the neck after age 30.

Bust: Small or medium, but measuring at least 2 inches less than the hip or thigh at their widest points. The **A** bust and shoulder form a narrow silhouette in comparison to the lower torso.

Back: Small or medium and less fleshy than the derriere.

Waist: Clearly defined or indented. The contrast between the **A** waist and full hip gives her figure its womanly appearance. The **A** rarely has problems with midriff bulge or pronounced "love handles" on the side. Short **A**'s are often short-waisted.

Hips: Always full in hip and derriere and frequently fuller still in the thigh. The **A** hip is almost always noticeably fuller at the low hip than at the high hip, and the tummy is often flat.

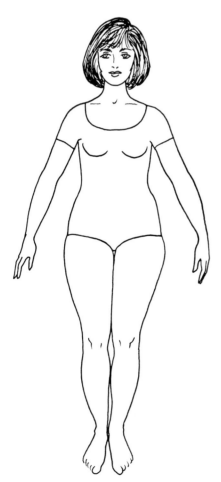

*The **A** figure is heavy in the hips and thighs.*

Thighs: Always full and frequently the widest visual line from front view. Cellulite or crepy skin on the hips, derriere, thighs and upper legs is common on the **A** body, and thigh bulge is her trademark.

Legs and Arms: Average or full in comparison to overall body size, with legs frequently heavier or more muscular-looking than arms. The **A** body is bottom-half heavy.

Best Features: Waist, bust, chin, midriff, back, and often, tummy and arms. (The **A** is the body type least prone to heart attacks.) **A**'s of medium or tall height often look slimmer than they are when dressed in styles that "skirt over" the heavy bottom, bringing the eye to the waistline and upper torso. Because of her natural curves, the **A** looks wonderfully female in sophisticated and womanly styles. Classic, career-suited looks are also good on the **A** figure.

Worst Features: Hips, thighs, legs, shoulder and derriere. The short **A** fears that she looks "underslung" because of her low center of gravity, and all **A**'s fear that bathing suits, pants, shorts and other lower-body-revealing clothes make them look pointedly triangular and out of balance.

℞ FOR DRESSING THE A

The most flattering lines for the **A** accomplish the following (an example is included for each point):

- Emphasize the midriff and waist (belts, waistbands and set-in waistbands).
- Broaden the upper torso—bust, arms and especially shoulder line (shoulder pads, full sleeves, eye-catching top details).
- De-emphasize the hips and thighs (dark bottoms, soft dirndls, full skirts).
- Create the illusion of top and bottom balance (poet-sleeved white shirt with dark mid-calf skirt).
- Emphasize the graceful back and neck and de-emphasize the derriere (sweaters, control-top hose and panty girdles).

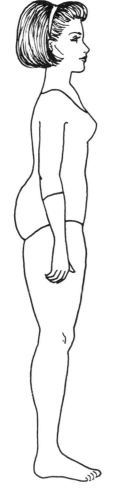

The A figure in profile.

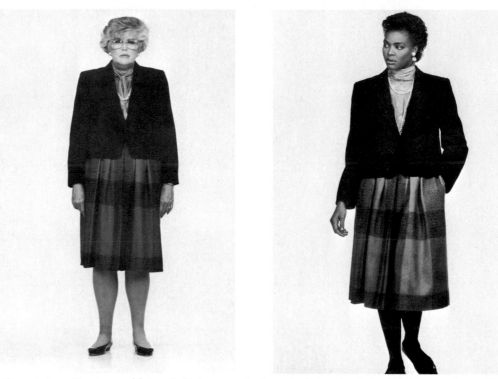

The suit is a disaster on **H** *Liz (left) because the boxy jacket ends at the hip bone and the skirt is full and short, making her look square all over. The same suit is wonderful on* **A** *Lucinda. The jacket fills out her upper torso and the skirt eases over her hip line.*

Following are lists of styles for **A**'s that emphasize the waist, broaden the shoulder line, and softly skirt over the hip and thigh area. All styles listed below as do's and don'ts for the **A** are illustrated in Chapter 7, *The* **H-O-A-X** *Glossary of Styles.*

THE BEST STYLES FOR **A** BODIES

DRESSES: THE BEST

Set-in waist dirndl	Sundress	Float
1-piece shirtdress	Strapless	Baby-doll smock
2-piece shirtdress	Longuette/Bustier	Bib dress
Elastic waist	V-yoke	Tent
Cinch waist	Peasant	Muu-muu
Surplice	Drop waist (slight)	Princess
Schoolgirl blouson	Drop waist (hip)	Coat dress (A-line)
Pinafore	Empire	Jumper
Prairie	Cocoon	A-line
Square dance		

The wide collar and padded-shoulder sweater-jacket create a horizontal line at Kaitlynn's shoulder, and her dirndl skirt defines her waist and slims the lower torso.

PANTS: THE BEST

Hip yoke	Jodhpur	Skort
Culotte	Jumpsuit	Wide-leg Bermuda
Pleated trousers	Wide-leg cuffed	Wide-leg walking
Palazzo	short	short
Harem	Tap pant	

SKIRTS: THE BEST

Wrap	Box pleat	Border print
Side pleat	Knife pleat	Hip yoke
A-line	Crystal pleat	Circle
Jean skirt	Kilt	Peasant
Modified dirndl	Gored	Bubble
Gaucho	High waist	Bell
Split	Flared/Semicircle	Tiered
Golf	Gathered	Handkerchief

Don't: Susan's dress droops at the shoulder and balloons everywhere else.

Do: Padded shoulders, a defined waist and eased, full skirt are more flattering to an **A**.

*Pat, an **A**, in a two-piece knit that has a broad shoulder line and falls in soft pleats over her hip/thigh line. The dark hose and shoes slim her legs and the round hat shape makes a soft frame for her face. A+ is more like it!*

COURTESY JEFF FLAX

TOPS: THE BEST

Bow	Collarless front	Pullover
Ruffled front	button	Crew
Poet/Victorian	Sport	Shell
Cossack	Polo	Turtleneck
Surplice	Button-down	Cowl
Notched/	Camp	Sweater vest
Convertible	Lumberjack	Fisherman
collar	Collarband	Sweatshirt
Peasant	Cardigan	T-shirt
Sailor		

COATS: THE BEST

Swagger	Balmacan	Trench
Cape	Smock	Redingote
Sherlock Holmes	Fling	Duster
cape	Princess	

JACKETS: THE BEST

Blazer	Spencer	Fly-away
Pea	Norfolk	Semifitted
Topper	Safari	Parka
Car coat	Peplum	Bolero jacket

*The leggings which are so good on the **O** are a disaster on the **A**. Gabrielle's **A** figure looks totally different in the dress with a soft, set-in waist, padded shoulders and circular skirt.*

A suit with an A-line skirt is right for Virginia, an **A**.

VESTS: THE BEST

Sweater vest	Waist coat	Bolero vest
Maude		

COLLARS & NECKLINES: THE BEST

Convertible	Bertha	Asymmetric
Button-down	Pierrot	Off-shoulder
Johnny	Bib	Scoop
Winged	Ruffle	Notched
Bermuda	Victorian	Shawl
Collarband	Drawstring	Portrait
Peter Pan	Jabot	Sailor
Crew	Bow	Cowl
Jewel	Batteau	Drape
Turtle	Teardrop	Grecian
Mandarin	Square	Tuxedo
Nehru	Sweetheart	Strapless
Cossack	Décolleté	

SLEEVES: THE BEST

Sleeveless	Cape	Pleated puff
Cap	Tulip	Gibson
Drop	Bell	Seven-eighths
Short	Dolman	Three-quarters
Baby doll	Batwing	Elbow
Puff	Bishop	Minimal
Flutter	Ruffled	Shirtsleeve
Carmen Miranda		

LINGERIE / FOUNDATIONS & DAYWEAR: THE BEST

Body briefer	Contour bra	Camisole
Merry widow	Sport bra	Teddy
Thigh panty girdle	Push-up bra	Brief
Capri girdle	(plunge or demi)	Tap pant
Boned girdle	Convertible bra	T-shirt
Corselette	Full slip	Shoulder pad
Soft-cup bra	Half slip	T-shirt
Underwire bra	Split petticoat	Hipster
Strapless bra	Petticoat	

Stirrup pants or leggings can work on an **A** *when the top is full and ends below the widest part of the thigh. Carolyn has also added big shoulder pads for balance.*
COURTESY BUTLER

Carolyn's bias-cut dress skims by her full hipline, but emphasizes her waistline.
COURTESY BUTLER

LINGERIE / AT HOME & SLEEPWEAR: THE BEST

Empire gown	Hostess coat	Robe (unbelted)
Granny gown	Bathrobe	Peignoir and
Caftan	Housecoat	negligee
Illusion caftan	Kimono	

SWIMWEAR: THE BEST

2-piece	Strapless	Sarong
Bikini	French cut	Gathered
Maillot	Dressmaker	Set-in skirt
Surplice	V-neck	Strapless maillot

THE WORST STYLES FOR A BODIES

DRESSES: THE WORST

Set-in waist sheath	Drop waist (thigh)	Tie front
Wrap	Flapper	Sheath
Peplum	Drop waist (elastic)	Chemise
2-piece blouson	Blouson	Shirtwaist chemise
Tunic dress	Drop blouson	Slip dress
Bubble	Fanny wrap	Tabard
2-piece overblouse	Thigh wrap	Sweater dress

PANTS: THE WORST

Straight leg	Toreador	Shorts
Peg leg	Pedal pusher	Boxer short
Stirrup	Short culotte	Jamaicas
Legging	Clam digger	Bermudas
Jean	Bell bottom	Walking short
Cropped	Overall	Romper
Capri	Short short	Pull-on elastic waist
Knicker		

SKIRTS: THE WORST

Straight	Inset pleat	Slit
Pegged/Hobble	Godet	Tube
Inverted pleat	Trumpet	Hipster
Kick pleat	Side slit	

Many A's are afraid to wear jeans, but Gabrielle has chosen a cut that fits properly, easing over her thigh line.

Diane, an A, in a baggy twill pant that minimizes her hip line. The vest and shirt add needed bulk to her upper torso.

TOPS: THE WORST

Blouson	Poor boy	Halter
Fanny wrap	Skimp	Camisole
Hip-yoke blouson	Tunic	Overblouse
V-neck cardigan	Tank	

COATS, JACKETS & VESTS: THE WORST

Fitted	Reefer	Battle jacket
Chesterfield	Slicker	Mao jacket
Quilted	Eton jacket	Nehru jacket
Shawl	Tuxedo	Wing-back jacket
Wrap	Stroller	Tabard vest
Polo/Overcoat		

COLLARS & NECKLINES: THE WORST

Halter	Halter vee	Camisole
V-neck	Keyhole	Chelsea

SLEEVES: THE WORST

Halter	Poet	Long fitted
Angel	Raglan	French cuff

Don't: The short skirt ends above the **A***'s wide upper leg, outlining the hip and thigh.*

Do: The V-yoke sundress with a soft dirndl skirt is a more flattering and grown-up summer look for **A***'s.*

LINGERIE: THE WORST

Waist cincher	Longline strapless	Shorty pajama
Control brief	bra	Sleepshirt
Panty girdle	Bikini	Oversize T-shirt
Longline bra	Baby doll	Pajama

SWIMWEAR: THE WORST

Boy leg	Tank	Jewel neck
Blouson	Halter	

SPECIAL NOTES FROM A SPECIAL **A**

Model and garment-center executive Susan Milano is a beautiful **A**. These are her recommendations:

- 2- and 3-piece outfits
- Full gathered trousers
- Stirrup pants with long full tunics
- Padded shoulders
- V-neck surplice dresses
- Dirndl skirts with blouses
- Full hairdos
- Glossy, colorful makeup
- Flapper dresses *with* big-shirt tops and padded shoulders
- Moderately oversized tops
- Sarong, dressmaker and French-cut bathing suits (French cut elongates legs)
- Skirts and tops for casual wear
- Belted overblouses (if not snug around hip/thigh area)
- Trench coats
- Big scarves
- Big earrings
- Belts, especially those with big buckles
- No boxy suits or straight skirts
- No thigh bands or clingy knits
- No jeans

6

The X Figure

DESCRIPTION: THE HOURGLASS FIGURE

Goal: To de-emphasize the exaggerated curviness of the figure while capitalizing on its innate softness, balance and womanliness. The X is blessed with the super femininity of her form, but must resist the temptation to dress in a pointedly sexy way. Such dressing literally "gilds the lily" of her natural womanliness and can actually make her look tacky.

DETAILS

The X body type has the following features:

Face: Usually oval, rectangular, heart-shaped or round with a well-defined chin or slight double chin. The X face size tends to be proportionate to overall body size.

Neck: Usually average in length, the X neck is rarely particularly short or long. The X usually has a slender but soft or fleshy nape, shoulder and collarbone area. Shoulders are medium, rarely broad or narrow.

Bust: Medium or large, with a lovely cleavage. The X breasts are pronounced and may make her appear top-heavy from profile view, but her bust measurement is not larger than her hip or she is an O. From front view, her shoulder and bust form a line that is fairly even with her widest hip line (no more than 2 inches larger in the hip).

Back: Medium or slightly small with a soft fleshy feeling to the shoulder-blade area.

Waist: Well-defined and small. The waist curves in from the midriff (which is not given to midriff bulge)

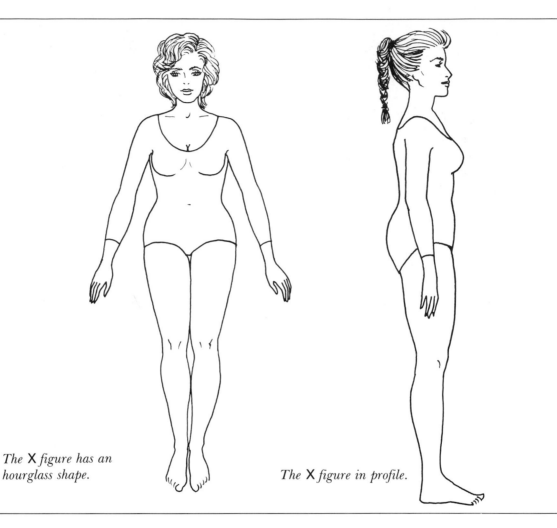

The X figure has an hourglass shape.

The X figure in profile.

and out to the high hip which is round. It clearly nips in from both front and side views.

Hips: Round and full, as is the derriere and tummy—although not so full as the A body. The biggest difference between the A and the X figures is in the hip and thigh area. The X hip is round and begins to curve in at the low hip as it approaches the thigh area. The low hip is the widest part of the lower torso.

Thighs: Full and fleshy, but narrower from the front view than the hipline. The X figure is prone to moderate inner- and outer-thigh bulge.

Legs and Arms: Like the torso, the X legs and arms are soft and shapely, usually average in size. With weight gain, X arms and upper legs tend toward chubbiness.

X *Alex in a high-drama dress with a set-in waist and draped skirt treatment.*
COURTESY JEFF FLAX

*Ruth is a mature **X** who is known for her style. One of her best looks is the belted two-piece "soft dressing" with coordinated hose and shoes.*
COURTESY ROYAL WOMAN

Best Features: Waist, bust, hips and back. The **X** is the most admired of female forms but is not always the easiest to dress because of its extreme curviness. The **X** looks wonderful and feminine in simple lines and soft fabrics, without fussiness or cuteness. Good separates and pared-down sophisticated dress silhouettes look good, as do career looks with blouses and tops that do not overemphasize the bust.

Worst Features: Thighs, upper arms, neck, chin, tummy and derriere, although these are usually minor problem areas for the **X**. Basically, she has the best-proportioned of all bodies. Finding and projecting her personal style is more important for the **X** than dressing to change the actual proportion of her shape.

The gathered cinch-waist dress is a figure disaster on the **H** *(left) with her straight middle, but lovely on the curvy* **X**.

℞ FOR DRESSING THE X

The most flattering lines for an **X** accomplish the following (an example is included for each point):

- Call attention to the waist and midriff (belts, cummerbunds, torso wraps).
- De-emphasize the bustline (non-clingy soft tops, dark tops).
- Emphasize the soft curve of the hip (soft dirndls, two-piece jersey dresses).
- Capitalize on the balance between top and bottom measurements (maillot bathing suits, jumpsuits).
- Drape softly over the back and neck (low-back cocktail dresses, cowl-neck loose-fitting sweaters).

THE BEST STYLES FOR X BODIES

Do: Simple curved lines like this princess coat-dress follow the curves of the X figure without being obvious.

DRESSES: THE BEST

Set-in waist sheath	Prairie	Tie front
Set-in waist dirndl	Square dance	Sheath
1-piece shirtdress	Sundress	Princess
2-piece shirtdress	Strapless	Coat dress
Elastic waist	Longuette/Bustier	Chemise
Cinch waist	V-yoke	Shirtwaist chemise
Surplice	Drop waist (slight)	Jumper
Wrap	Drop waist (hip)	Slip dress
Peplum	Drop waist (thigh)	Sweater dress
Schoolgirl blouson	Flapper	A-line
Pinafore	Fanny wrap	Tunic dress

Don't: Sexy, cutesy looks are tacky on the ultra-curvy X body.

PANTS: THE BEST

Straight leg	Short culotte	Wide-leg cuffed
Peg leg	Culotte	short
Stirrup	Clam digger	Tap pant
Legging	Pleated trousers	Boxer short
Jean	Bell bottom	Skort
Cropped	Harem	Jamaicas
Knicker	Jodhpur	Bermudas
Toreador	Jumpsuit	Walking short
Pedal pusher	Short short	Romper
Hip yoke	Shorts	

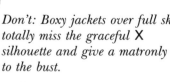

Don't: Boxy jackets over full skirts totally miss the graceful X silhouette and give a matronly look to the bust.

SKIRTS: THE BEST

Straight	Gaucho	Gathered
Pegged/Hobble	Split	Border print
Inverted pleat	Golf	Hip yoke
Kick pleat	Hipster	Circle
Wrap	Box pleat	Peasant
Inset pleat	Knife pleat	Bubble
Godet	Crystal pleat	Bell
Trumpet	Kilt	Tiered
A-line	Gored	Handkerchief
Jean skirt	High waist	Side pleat
Modified dirndl	Flared/Semicircle	

*Rae is a full-busted **X** who likes broad shoulders and simple lines. The shoulder treatment here minimizes her bust.*

TOPS: THE BEST

Bow	Polo	Poor boy
Poet/Victorian	Button-down	Turtleneck
Cossack	Camp	Cowl
Surplice	Lumberjack	Sweater vest
Notched/	Collarband	Fisherman
Convertible	Cardigan	Tank
collar	V-neck cardigan	Halter
Collarless front	Pullover	Camisole
button	Crew	Overblouse
Sport	Shell	T-shirt

COATS: THE BEST

Swagger	Fitted	Shawl
Cape	Princess	Wrap
Sherlock Holmes	Trench	Polo/Overcoat
cape	Redingote	Reefer
Balmacan	Chesterfield	Slicker
Fling	Quilted	Duster

JACKETS: THE BEST

Blazer	Tuxedo	Parka
Pea	Norfolk	Battle jacket
Topper	Safari	Bolero jacket
Car coat	Peplum	Mao
Eton	Semifitted	Nehru
Spencer	Stroller	

VESTS: THE BEST

Sweater vest	Waist coat	Bolero vest

COLLARS & NECKLINES: THE BEST

Convertible	Bertha	Keyhole
Button-down	Pierrot	Camisole
Johnny	Bib	Asymmetric
Winged	Ruffle	Off-shoulder
Bermuda	Victorian	Notched
Collarband	Drawstring	Chelsea
Peter Pan	Jabot	Shawl
Crew	Bow	Portrait
Jewel	Batteau	Sailor
Halter	V-neck	Cowl
Turtle	Teardrop	Drape
Mandarin	Square	Grecian
Nehru	Sweethcart	Tuxedo
Cossack	Halter vee	Strapless

SLEEVES: THE BEST

Cap	Tulip	Gibson
Drop	Bell	Raglan
Short	Angel	Long fitted
Baby doll	Dolman	Seven-eighths
Puff	Batwing	Three-quarters
Flutter	Poet	Elbow
Carmen Miranda	Bishop	Minimal
Cape	Ruffled	Shirtsleeve
Halter	Pleated puff	French cuff

Lill can wear glamorama, but like most well-dressed **X** *women, she knows intuitively not to "gild the lily" with overdone accessories.*

LINGERIE / FOUNDATIONS & DAYWEAR: THE BEST

Body briefer	Push-up bra	Teddy
Merry widow	(plunge or demi)	Bikini
Control brief	Convertible bra	Brief
Panty girdle	Full slip	Tap pant
Thigh panty girdle	Half slip	T-shirt
Underwire bra	Split petticoat	Shoulder pad
Strapless bra	Petticoat	T-shirt
Sport bra	Camisole	Hipster

The slip dress and cummerbund work well on X Karen as they define her figure without exaggerating it.

COURTESY JEFF FLAX

LINGERIE / AT HOME & SLEEPWEAR: THE BEST

Baby doll	Empire gown	Bathrobe
Shorty pajama	Granny gown	Kimono
Sleepshirt	Illusion caftan	Peignoir and
Oversize T-shirt	Hostess coat	negligee
Pajama		

SWIMWEAR: THE BEST

2-piece	Strapless	V-neck
Bikini	French cut	Jewel neck
Maillot	Tank	Gathered
Surplice	Halter	Set-in skirt
Boy leg		

THE WORST STYLES FOR X BODIES

DRESSES: THE WORST

Peasant	Blouson	Baby-doll smock
2-piece blouson	Drop blouson	Bib dress
Bubble	Thigh wrap	Tent
2-piece overblouse	Cocoon	Muu-muu
Drop waist (elastic)	Float	Tabard
Empire		

PANTS: THE WORST

Capri	Overall	Wide-leg walking
Palazzo	Wide-leg Bermuda	short

SKIRTS: THE WORST

Side slit	Slit	Tube

TOPS: THE WORST

Ruffled front	Fanny wrap	Skimp
Peasant	Sailor	Tunic
Blouson	Hip-yoke blouson	Sweatshirt

X Tara says her number one "no-no" is a tight sweater.

COATS, JACKETS & VESTS: THE WORST

Smock	Wing-back jacket	Maude vest
Fly-away jacket	Tabard vest	

COLLARS, NECKLINES & SLEEVES: THE WORST

Décolleté	Scoop	Sleeveless

LINGERIE: THE WORST

Waist cincher	Soft-cup bra	Contour bra
Capri girdle	Longline bra	Caftan
Boned girdle	Longline strapless	Housecoat
Corselette	bra	Robe (unbelted)

SWIMWEAR: THE WORST

Blouson	Sarong	Strapless maillot
Dressmaker		

SPECIAL NOTES FROM A SPECIAL X

Model Tara Robinson is a beautiful, curvy X. Here is what she recommends:

- Good, supportive bras
- Shoulder pads
- Waist accents
- Softly draped—but never clingy—fabrics
- Control-top pantyhose
- V necklines
- Shirts with plackets
- Pleated trousers
- Two-piece dresses
- Set-in waistbands
- No boxy or matronly looks
- No blatantly sexy looks
- No tight clothes
- No tops that fall straight off the bust as if it were a shelf
- Standing up straight, but *not* the "breasts forward/only woman on earth" posture.

Tara's figure is so curvy that the last thing she needs is a blatantly sexy dress. Simple and understated works best for her.

7

The H-O-A-X *Glossary of Styles*

THIS CHAPTER is a comprehensive, illustrated glossary of garment styles representing fashions of the present, past and future (inevitably). Every garment is labeled with its name and the letters of the body types that look best in it. Footnotes appear above certain letters where there are specific exceptions or suggestions.

Garments and details are arranged in the glossary by the following categories:

- Dresses
- Pants
- Skirts
- Tops
- Coats and jackets
- Collars and necklines
- Sleeves
- Lingerie
- Swimsuits

Suits are not listed separately because each is a combination of a jacket and skirt or pants.

Following the illustrated glossary are charts summarizing the information for quick, easy reference. Each chart covers one category of garment and has a checklist of the body types most appropriate for each style.

In some cases, garments are not checked for a body type because they cover up a particularly good feature of the body type, *not* because they look bad. For instance, boxy jackets miss the small waist of an **X**, and wide-leg pants miss the slender thighs of an **O**. More often, however, the garment is not checked because it is unflattering as it brings attention to a negative feature of the body type.

For example, the *wing-back jacket* is listed for the **O** because it has torso fullness. It is not listed for the **H** or **X** because it is too boxy, or for the **A** because it draws the eye out at the hip. The *side-pleated skirt* is good on the **H**, **A** and **X** bodies because it eases over the tummy and high hip. It is not listed for the **O** because it has too much volume and defines the waist.

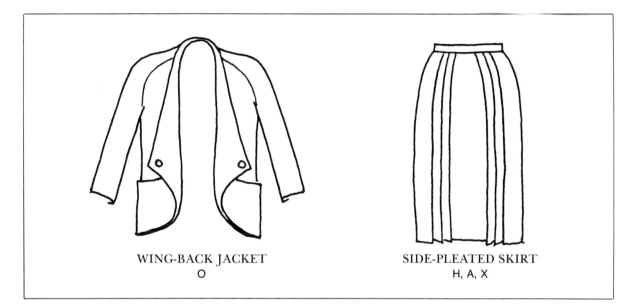

WING-BACK JACKET
O

SIDE-PLEATED SKIRT
H, A, X

Chapter 9, *Shaping Your Body with Color, Texture and Line,* will explain the visual theory—or the whys and wherefores—behind my thinking.

Exceptions to every rule *do* occur, and you should use your eye and common sense. Be willing to try on something you like that is *not* recommended for your body type to see if you can make it work. For instance, cardigan sweater vests will work for all body types if they are worn open or with a jacket over them. Also, pullovers worn oversized with shoulder pads will work on the **O** where traditional pullovers will not.

DRESSES / WAIST EMPHASIS

SET-IN WAIST SHEATH
X

SET-IN WAIST DIRNDL
A, X

1-PIECE SHIRTDRESS
A, X

2-PIECE SHIRTDRESS
H, O^1, A, X

ELASTIC WAIST
H, A^2, X

CINCH WAIST
A^2, X

See footnotes on page 74.

DRESSES / WAIST EMPHASIS

SURPLICE
A, X

WRAP
X

PEPLUM
X

PINAFORE
A, X

SCHOOLGIRL BLOUSON
A, X

DRESSES / WAIST EMPHASIS

PRAIRIE
A, X

SQUARE DANCE
A, X

SUNDRESS
A³, X

STRAPLESS
A³, X

LONGUETTE/BUSTIER
A³, X

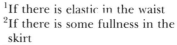

¹If there is elastic in the waist
²If there is some fullness in the skirt
³A's with *very* narrow shoulders should avoid these shoulder-baring dresses.

DRESSES / HORIZONTAL LINE NOT AT WAIST

V-YOKE
H, A¹, X

PEASANT
H², A

2-PIECE BLOUSON
H, O

TUNIC DRESS
H, O, X

BUBBLE
H, O

2-PIECE OVERBLOUSE
H, O

See footnotes on page 77.

DRESSES / HORIZONTAL LINE NOT AT WAIST

DROP WAIST (SLIGHT)
A, X

DROP WAIST (HIP)
H, O, A¹, X

DROP WAIST (THIGH)
H, O, X

FLAPPER
H, O, X

DROP WAIST (ELASTIC)
H, O

EMPIRE
H, A

See footnotes on page 77.

DRESSES / HORIZONTAL LINE NOT AT WAIST

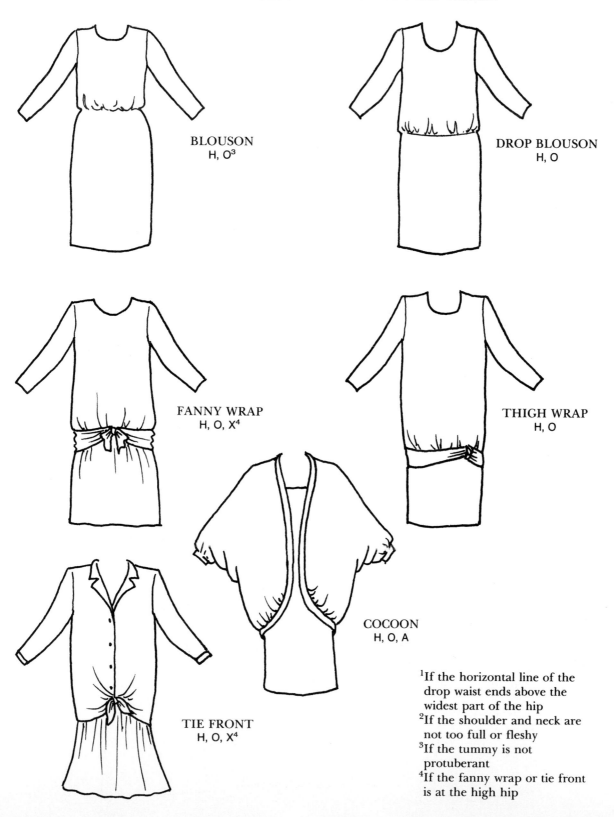

BLOUSON
H, O[3]

DROP BLOUSON
H, O

FANNY WRAP
H, O, X[4]

THIGH WRAP
H, O

COCOON
H, O, A

TIE FRONT
H, O, X[4]

[1]If the horizontal line of the
 drop waist ends above the
 widest part of the hip
[2]If the shoulder and neck are
 not too full or fleshy
[3]If the tummy is not
 protuberant
[4]If the fanny wrap or tie front
 is at the high hip

DRESSES / NO WAIST

FLOAT
H, O, A

BABY-DOLL SMOCK
A^1

BIB DRESS
H^2, O^2, A

TENT
A

MUU-MUU
H^2, O^2, A

See footnotes on page 80.

DRESSES / NO WAIST

SHEATH
H^2, X

PRINCESS
H^3, A, X

COAT
H^3, A^4, X

CHEMISE
H, O^3, X

SHIRTWAIST CHEMISE
H^3, O^3, X

See footnotes on page 80.

DRESSES / NO WAIST

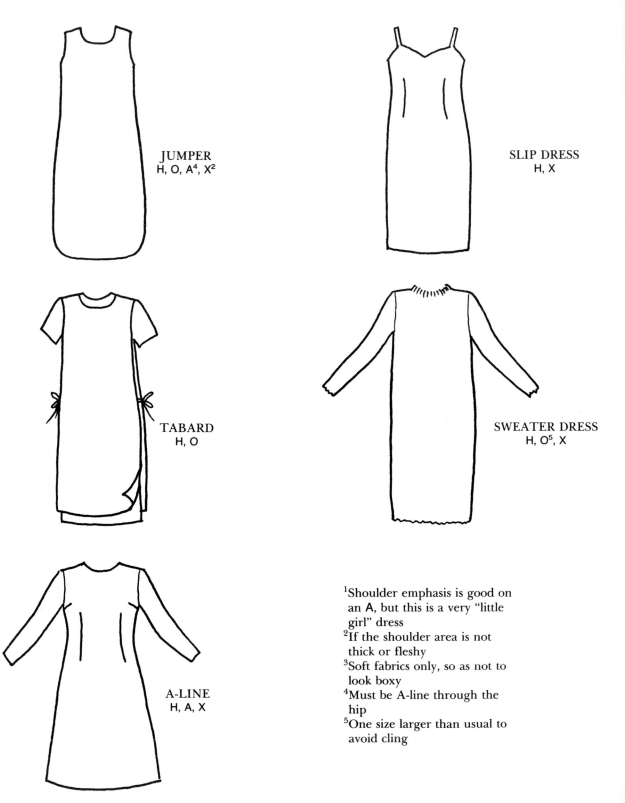

JUMPER
H, O, A^4, X^2

SLIP DRESS
H, X

TABARD
H, O

SWEATER DRESS
H, O^5, X

A-LINE
H, A, X

[1]Shoulder emphasis is good on an **A**, but this is a very "little girl" dress
[2]If the shoulder area is not thick or fleshy
[3]Soft fabrics only, so as not to look boxy
[4]Must be A-line through the hip
[5]One size larger than usual to avoid cling

PANTS / NARROW

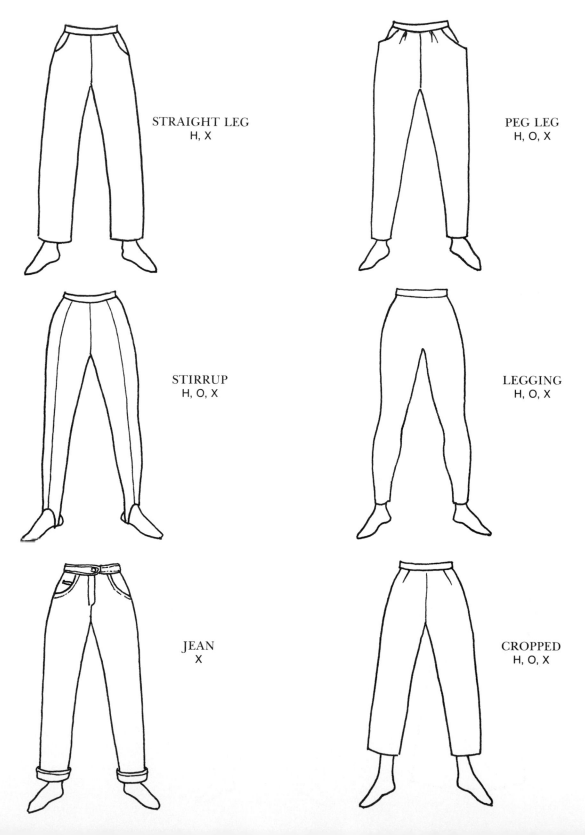

STRAIGHT LEG
H, X

PEG LEG
H, O, X

STIRRUP
H, O, X

LEGGING
H, O, X

JEAN
X

CROPPED
H, O, X

PANTS / NARROW

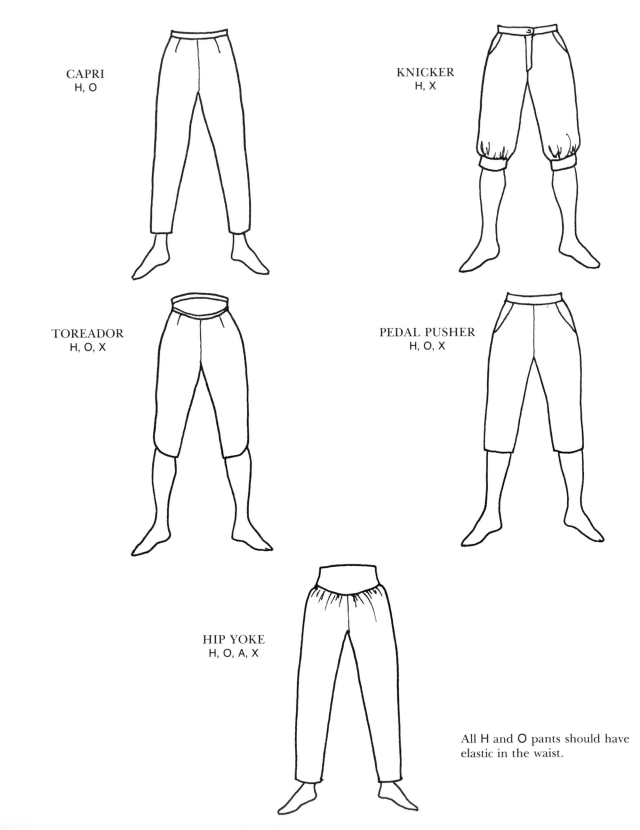

CAPRI
H, O

KNICKER
H, X

TOREADOR
H, O, X

PEDAL PUSHER
H, O, X

HIP YOKE
H, O, A, X

All H and O pants should have
elastic in the waist.

PANTS / FULL

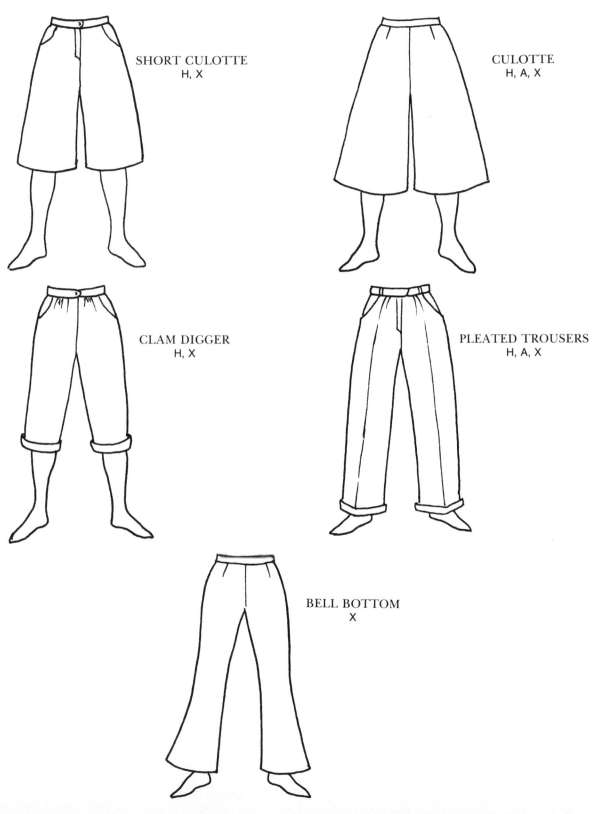

SHORT CULOTTE
H, X

CULOTTE
H, A, X

CLAM DIGGER
H, X

PLEATED TROUSERS
H, A, X

BELL BOTTOM
X

PANTS / FULL

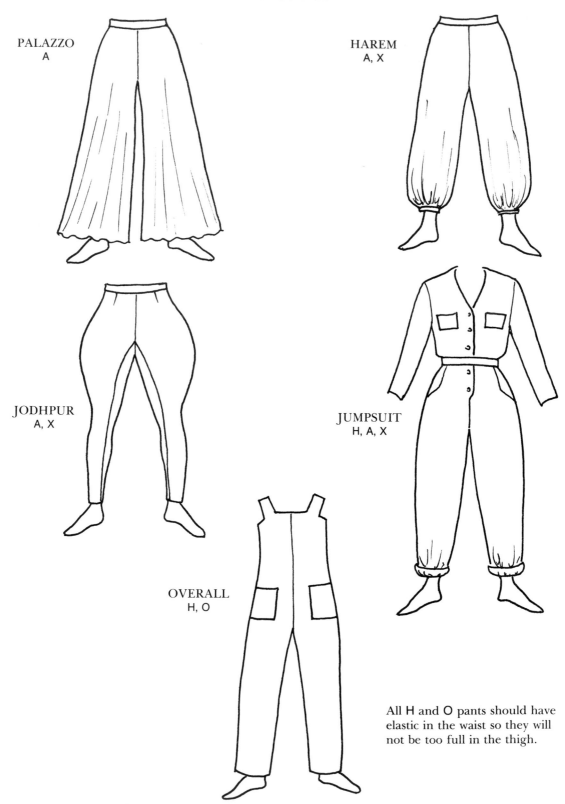

PALAZZO
A

HAREM
A, X

JODHPUR
A, X

JUMPSUIT
H, A, X

OVERALL
H, O

All **H** and **O** pants should have
elastic in the waist so they will
not be too full in the thigh.

SHORTS

SHORT SHORT
H^1, O^1, X

SHORTS
H^1, O^1, X

WIDE-LEG CUFFED
H^2, O^2, A^3, X

TAP PANT
H^2, O^2, A^3, X

BOXER
H^2, O, X

SKORT
H^2, O^2, A, X

See footnotes on page 86.

SHORTS

JAMAICA
H², O², X

BERMUDA
H², O², X

WALKING SHORT
H², X

WIDE-LEG BERMUDA
A³

WIDE-LEG WALKING SHORT
H, A

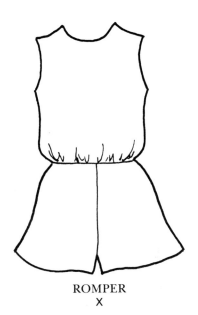

ROMPER
X

¹If legs are good
²With elastic waist
³If they end below the biggest part of the thigh

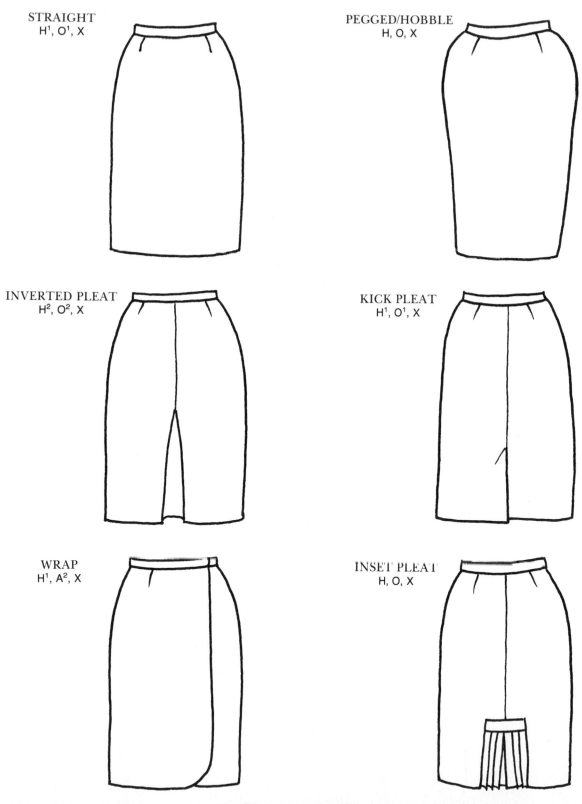

STRAIGHT
H¹, O¹, X

PEGGED/HOBBLE
H, O, X

INVERTED PLEAT
H², O², X

KICK PLEAT
H¹, O¹, X

WRAP
H¹, A², X

INSET PLEAT
H, O, X

See footnotes on page 89.

SKIRTS / NARROW

GODET
H³, O³, X

TRUMPET
H³, O³, X

A-LINE
H, A, X

JEAN SKIRT
H, A, X

SIDE SLIT
H, O³

SLIT
H¹, O³

SKIRTS / NARROW

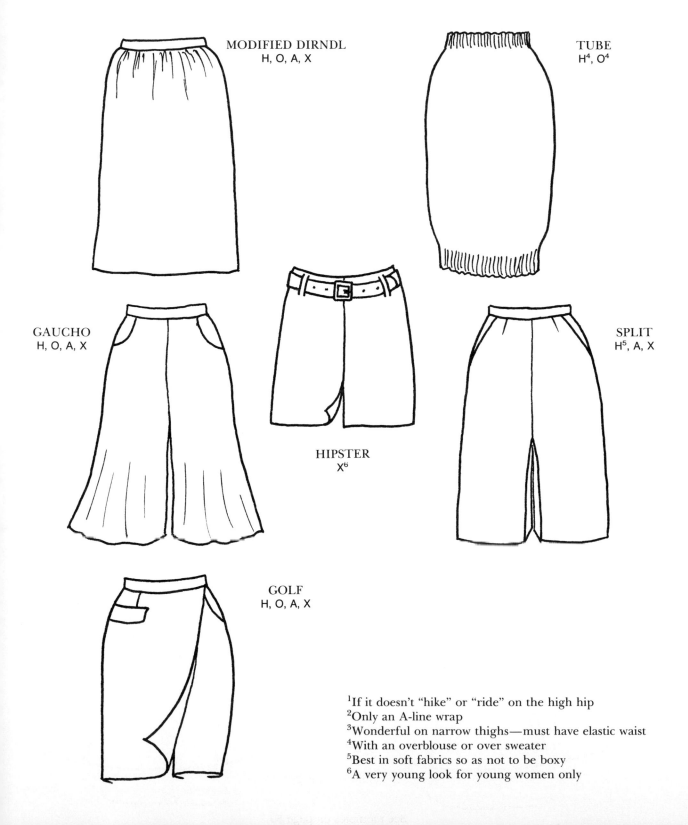

MODIFIED DIRNDL
H, O, A, X

TUBE
H[4], O[4]

GAUCHO
H, O, A, X

HIPSTER
X[6]

SPLIT
H[5], A, X

GOLF
H, O, A, X

[1]If it doesn't "hike" or "ride" on the high hip
[2]Only an A-line wrap
[3]Wonderful on narrow thighs—must have elastic waist
[4]With an overblouse or over sweater
[5]Best in soft fabrics so as not to be boxy
[6]A very young look for young women only

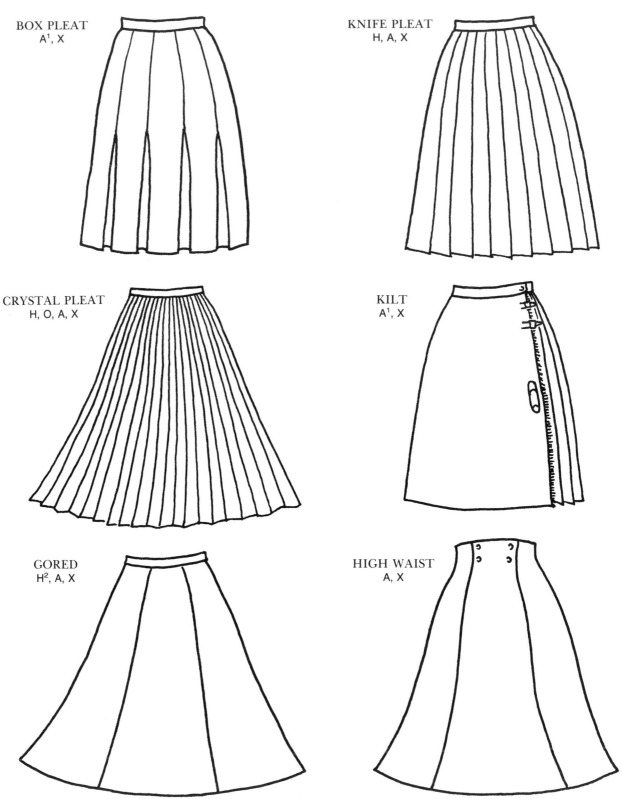

BOX PLEAT
A[1], X

KNIFE PLEAT
H, A, X

CRYSTAL PLEAT
H, O, A, X

KILT
A[1], X

GORED
H[2], A, X

HIGH WAIST
A, X

See footnotes on page 92.

FLARED/SEMICIRCLE
A, X

GATHERED
A, X

BORDER PRINT
H, O, A, X

HIP YOKE
H^2, O^3, A^4, X

CIRCLE
A, X

See footnotes on page 92.

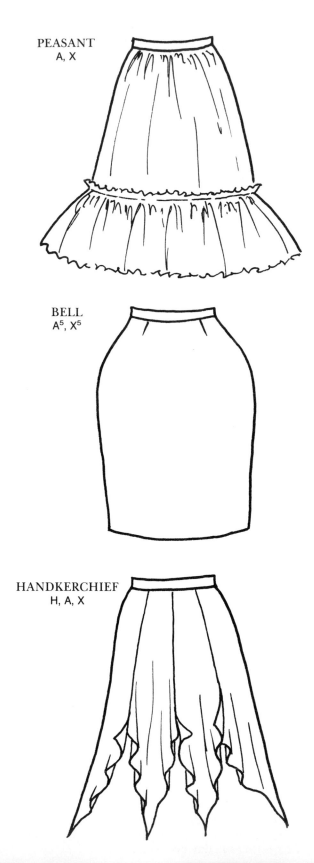

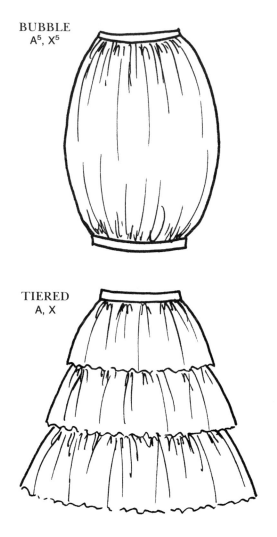

PEASANT
A, X

BUBBLE
A⁵, X⁵

BELL
A⁵, X⁵

TIERED
A, X

HANDKERCHIEF
H, A, X

[1]If stitching of pleat ends well above the wide part of the hipline
[2]If there is elastic in the waist
[3]Same as [2], but with an overblouse
[4]If the yoke ends above the widest part of the hip
[5]A very young look for young women only

BOW
H, A, X

RUFFLED FRONT
O, A

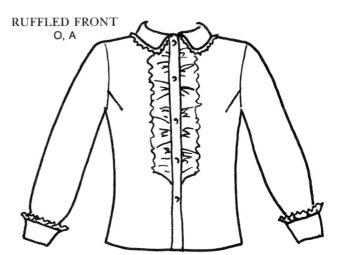

POET/VICTORIAN
H, A, X

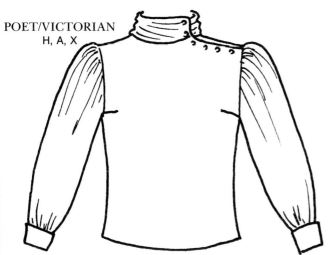

COSSACK
A, X

SURPLICE
A, X

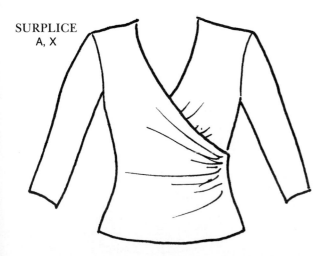

PEASANT
H[1], A

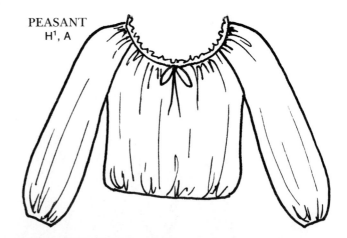

[1]If shoulders are not very fleshy
[2]If upper torso is very heavy, softer blouses are preferable
[3]Best worn as middy overblouse

TOPS / BLOUSES

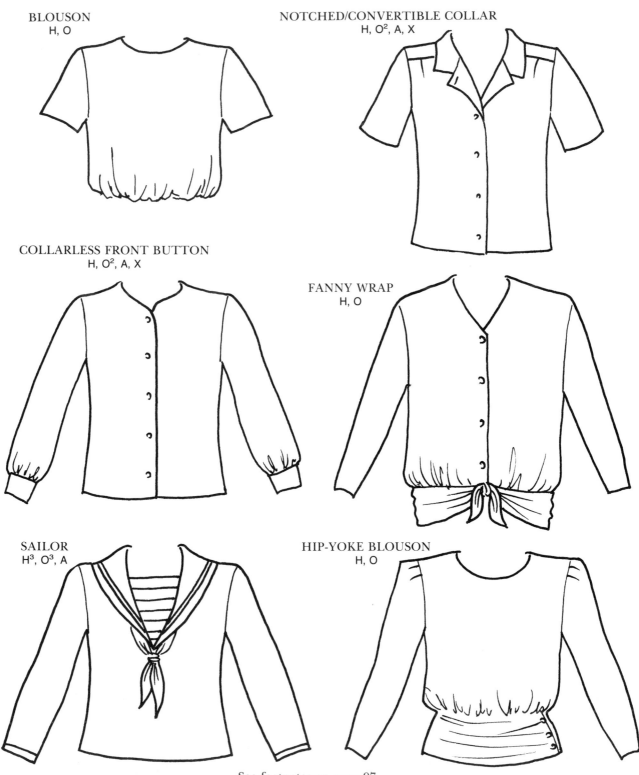

BLOUSON
H, O

NOTCHED/CONVERTIBLE COLLAR
H, O², A, X

COLLARLESS FRONT BUTTON
H, O², A, X

FANNY WRAP
H, O

SAILOR
H³, O³, A

HIP-YOKE BLOUSON
H, O

See footnotes on page 97.

TOPS / SHIRTS

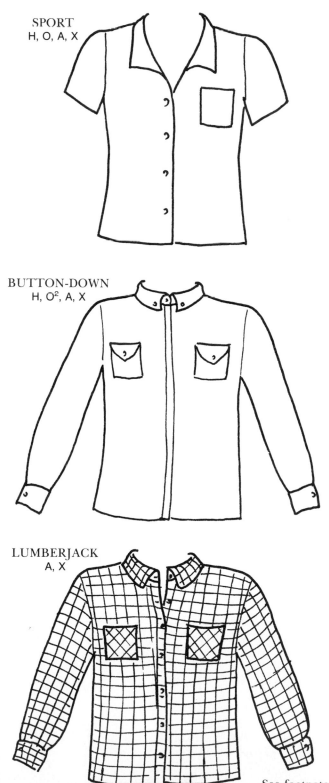

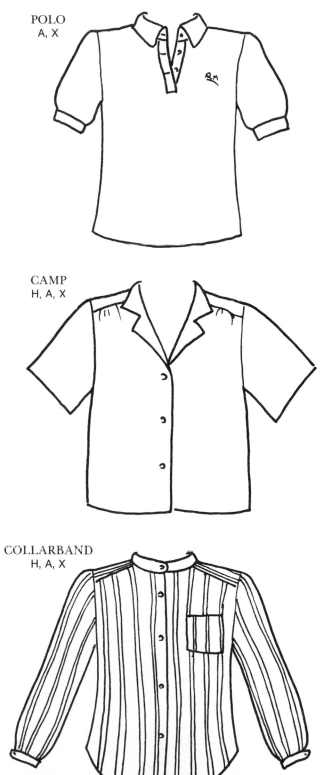

SPORT
H, O, A, X

POLO
A, X

BUTTON-DOWN
H, O², A, X

CAMP
H, A, X

LUMBERJACK
A, X

COLLARBAND
H, A, X

See footnotes on page 97.

CARDIGAN
H, O^1, A^1, X

V-NECK CARDIGAN
H, O^2, X

PULLOVER
H, A, X

CREW
H, A, X

SHELL
H, A, X

SKIMP
H, O

See footnotes on page 97.

POOR BOY
X

TURTLENECK
A³, X

COWL
H, O, A, X

TUNIC
H, O

SWEATER VEST
H, A, X

FISHERMAN
A, X

¹Unbuttoned
²Must be loose—oversized works well
³With shoulder pads

TOPS / MISCELLANEOUS

TANK
H, X

HALTER
X

CAMISOLE
H, X

SWEATSHIRT
H, O, A

OVERBLOUSE
H, O, X

T-SHIRT
H, A, X

COATS / FULL

SWAGGER
A, X

CAPE
H, O, A, X

SHERLOCK HOLMES CAPE
H, O, A, X

BALMACAN
A, X

SMOCK
H, O, A

FLING
H, O, A, X

COATS / NARROW

FITTED
H, X

PRINCESS
A, X

TRENCH
H, A, X

REDINGOTE
A, X

CHESTERFIELD
H, O, X

QUILTED
H[1], X

[1]Not on a very short body

COATS / NARROW

SHAWL
H, X

WRAP
H, X

POLO/OVERCOAT
H, O, X

REEFER
H, X

SLICKER
H, O, X

DUSTER
H, O, A, X

JACKETS

BLAZER
H, A, X

PEA
H, O, A¹, X

TOPPER
H, O, A¹, X

CAR COAT
H, O, A¹, X

ETON
H, X

SPENCER
H, A, X

See footnotes on page 104.

JACKETS

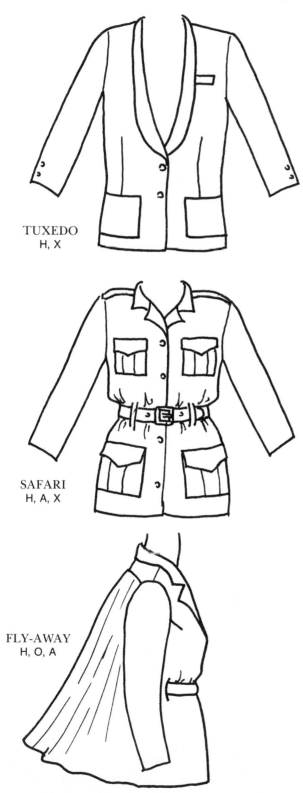

TUXEDO
H, X

SAFARI
H, A, X

FLY-AWAY
H, O, A

NORFOLK
H, A, X

PEPLUM
A, X

SEMIFITTED
H, O², A, X

See footnotes on page 104.

STROLLER
H, O, X

PARKA
H, O, A¹, X

BATTLE JACKET
H, O, X

BOLERO
A, X

MAO
H, O, X

NEHRU
H, X

¹If it ends below the widest part of the hip and fits with ease over the hip and thigh area
²Unbuttoned if very busty

SWEATER VEST
H, A, X

TABARD
H, O

MAUDE
H, O, A

WAIST COAT
A, X

BOLERO VEST
A, X

COLLARS AND NECKLINES / HIGH EMPHASIS

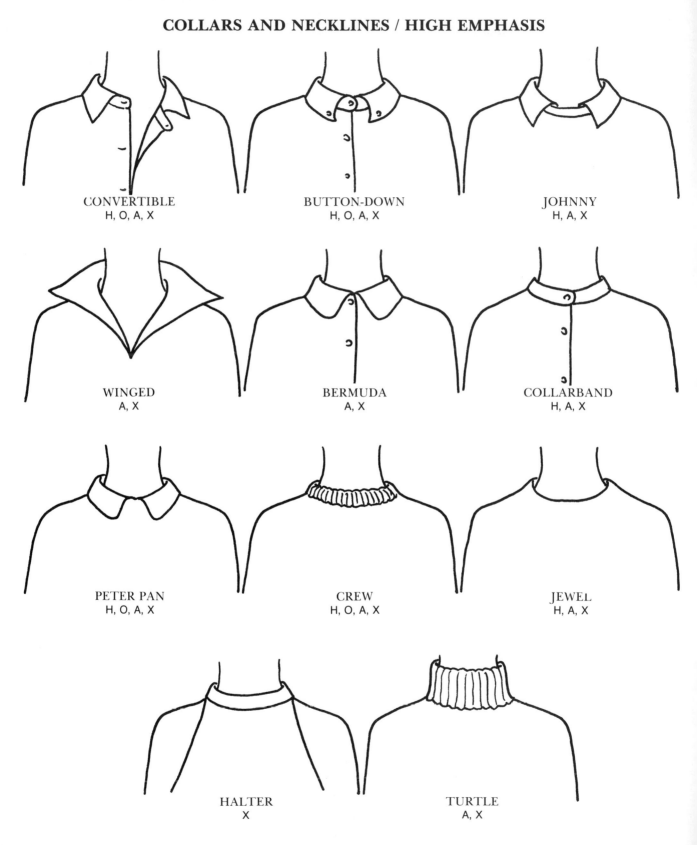

CONVERTIBLE
H, O, A, X

BUTTON-DOWN
H, O, A, X

JOHNNY
H, A, X

WINGED
A, X

BERMUDA
A, X

COLLARBAND
H, A, X

PETER PAN
H, O, A, X

CREW
H, O, A, X

JEWEL
H, A, X

HALTER
X

TURTLE
A, X

COLLARS AND NECKLINES / HIGH EMPHASIS

MANDARIN
A, X

NEHRU
A, X

COSSACK
A, X

BERTHA
A, X

PIERROT
A, X

BIB
A, X

RUFFLE
A, X

VICTORIAN
A, X

DRAWSTRING
H, A, X

JABOT
H, A, X

BOW
H, A, X

BATTEAU
H, A, X

COLLARS AND NECKLINES / LOW EMPHASIS

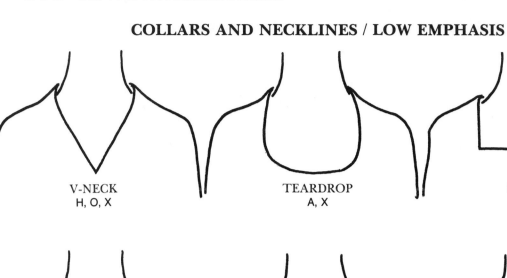

V-NECK
H, O, X

TEARDROP
A, X

SQUARE
A, X

SWEETHEART
H, A, X

HALTER VEE
X

DÈCOLLETÈ
H, O, A

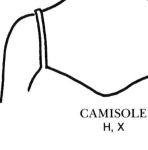

KEYHOLE
H, X

CAMISOLE
H, X

ASYMMETRIC
H, A, X

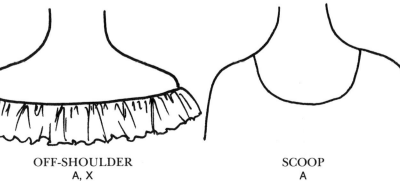

OFF-SHOULDER
A, X

SCOOP
A

COLLARS AND NECKLINES / LOW EMPHASIS

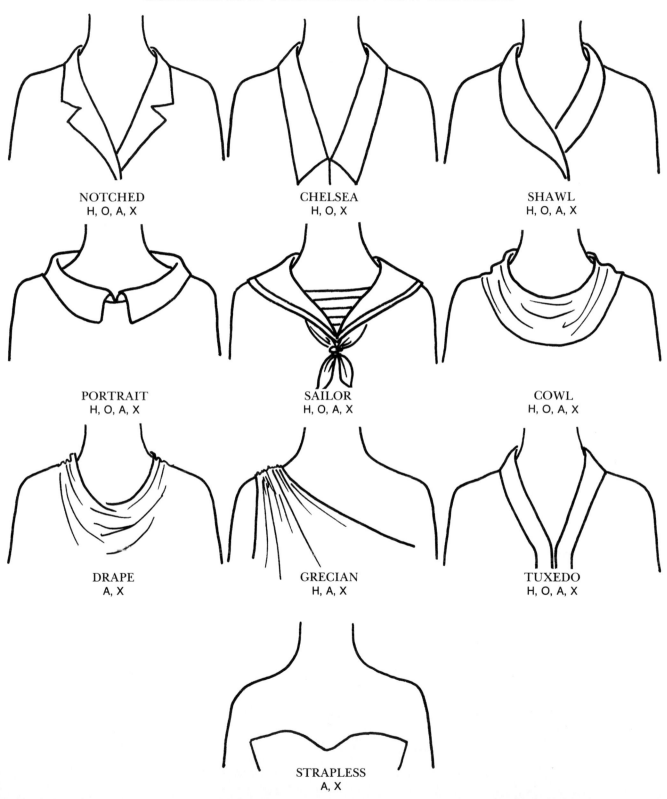

NOTCHED
H, O, A, X

CHELSEA
H, O, X

SHAWL
H, O, A, X

PORTRAIT
H, O, A, X

SAILOR
H, O, A, X

COWL
H, O, A, X

DRAPE
A, X

GRECIAN
H, A, X

TUXEDO
H, O, A, X

STRAPLESS
A, X

SLEEVES / BARE

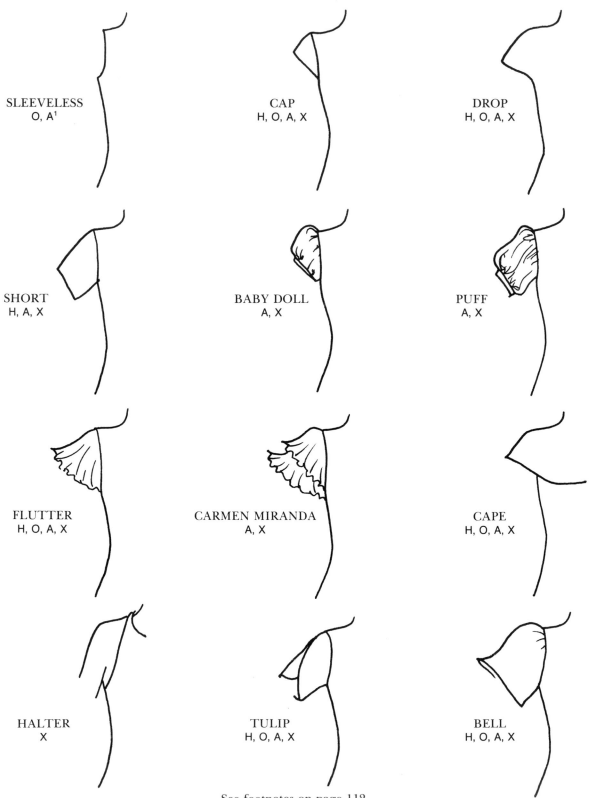

SLEEVELESS
O, A[1]

CAP
H, O, A, X

DROP
H, O, A, X

SHORT
H, A, X

BABY DOLL
A, X

PUFF
A, X

FLUTTER
H, O, A, X

CARMEN MIRANDA
A, X

CAPE
H, O, A, X

HALTER
X

TULIP
H, O, A, X

BELL
H, O, A, X

See footnotes on page 112.

SLEEVES / FULL

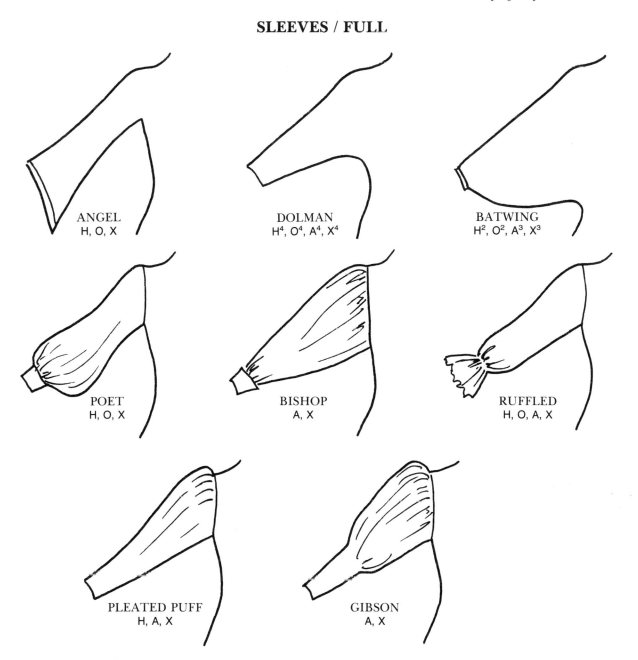

ANGEL
H, O, X

DOLMAN
H⁴, O⁴, A⁴, X⁴

BATWING
H², O², A³, X³

POET
H, O, X

BISHOP
A, X

RUFFLED
H, O, A, X

PLEATED PUFF
H, A, X

GIBSON
A, X

SLEEVES / NARROW

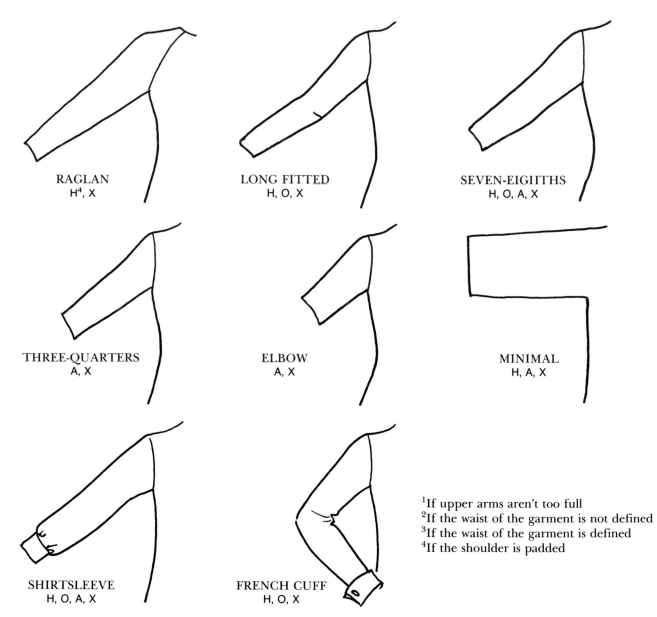

RAGLAN
H⁴, X

LONG FITTED
H, O, X

SEVEN-EIGHTHS
H, O, A, X

THREE-QUARTERS
A, X

ELBOW
A, X

MINIMAL
H, A, X

SHIRTSLEEVE
H, O, A, X

FRENCH CUFF
H, O, X

[1]If upper arms aren't too full
[2]If the waist of the garment is not defined
[3]If the waist of the garment is defined
[4]If the shoulder is padded

LINGERIE / FOUNDATIONS

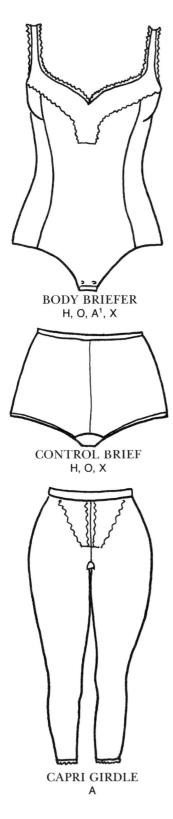

BODY BRIEFER
H, O, A[1], X

CONTROL BRIEF
H, O, X

CAPRI GIRDLE
A

MERRY WIDOW
H, O, A, X

PANTY GIRDLE
X

BONED GIRDLE
A[2]

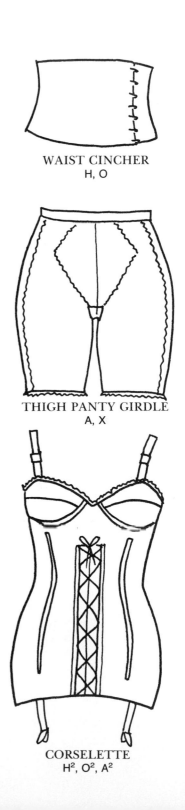

WAIST CINCHER
H, O

THIGH PANTY GIRDLE
A, X

CORSELETTE
H[2], O[2], A[2]

See footnotes on page 115.

LINGERIE / FOUNDATIONS

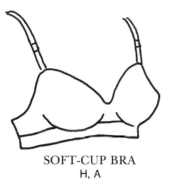

SOFT-CUP BRA
H, A

UNDERWIRE BRA
H, O, A, X

STRAPLESS BRA
A, X

LONGLINE BRA
H, O

LONGLINE STRAPLESS BRA
H, O

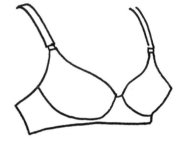

CONTOUR BRA
H, A

SPORT BRA
H, A, X

PUSH-UP BRA (PLUNGE OR DEMI)
H, A, X

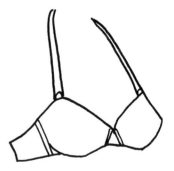

CONVERTIBLE BRA
H, A, X

LINGERIE / DAYWEAR

FULL SLIP
H, O, A, X

PETTICOAT
A, X

HALF SLIP
H, O, A, X

CAMISOLE
H, O, A, X

BRIEF
H, O, A, X

SPLIT PETTICOAT
H, O, A, X

TEDDY
H, O, A, X

TAP PANT
H, O, A, X

BIKINI
X³

SHOULDER PAD
H, O, A, X

HIPSTER
A, X

T-SHIRT
A, X

¹If it is loose in the leg band
²An old-fashioned and unattractive garment
³If the hipline is not very fleshy

BABY DOLL
H, O, X

SHORTY PAJAMA
H, O, X

SLEEPSHIRT
H, O, X

OVERSIZE T-SHIRT
H, O, X

PAJAMA
H, X

EMPIRE GOWN
H, A, X

GRANNY GOWN
H, O, A, X

CAFTAN
H, O, A

ILLUSION CAFTAN
H, O, A, X

HOSTESS COAT
H, O, A, X

BATHROBE
A, X

HOUSECOAT
H, O, A

KIMONO
H, A, X

ROBE
H, O, A

PEIGNOIR & NEGLIGEE
H, O, A, X

SWIMWEAR

2-PIECE
A, X

BIKINI
A, X

MAILLOT
H, O, A, X

SURPLICE
A, X

BOY LEG
H, O, X

STRAPLESS
H, A, X

BLOUSON
H, O

FRENCH CUT
H, O, A, X

DRESSMAKER
A

SWIMWEAR

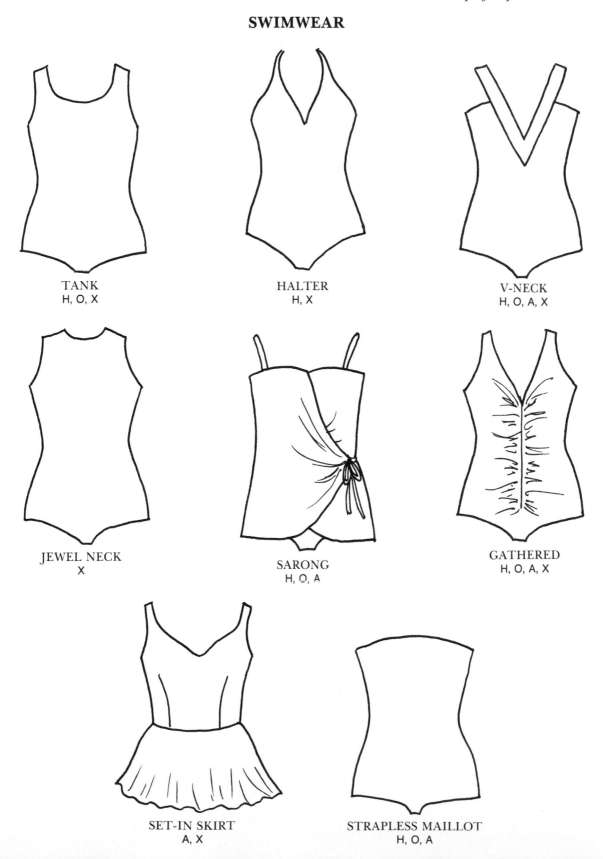

TANK
H, O, X

HALTER
H, X

V-NECK
H, O, A, X

JEWEL NECK
X

SARONG
H, O, A

GATHERED
H, O, A, X

SET-IN SKIRT
A, X

STRAPLESS MAILLOT
H, O, A

DRESSES (WAIST EMPHASIS)

	H	O	A	X
Set-in waist sheath				√
Set-in waist dirndl			√	√
1-piece shirtdress			√	√
2-piece shirtdress	√	√[1]	√	√
Elastic waist	√		√[2]	√
Cinch waist			√[2]	√
Surplice			√	√
Wrap				√
Peplum				√
Schoolgirl blouson			√	√
Pinafore			√	√
Prairie			√	√
Square dance			√	√
Sundress			√[3]	√
Strapless			√[3]	√
Longuette/Bustier			√[3]	√

[1]If there is elastic in the waist
[2]If there is some fullness in the skirt
[3]A's with *very* narrow shoulders should avoid these
shoulder-baring dresses

DRESSES (HORIZONTAL LINE NOT AT WAIST)

	H	O	A	X
V-yoke	√		√[1]	√
Peasant	√[2]		√	
2-piece blouson	√	√		
Tunic dress	√	√		√
Bubble	√	√		
2-piece overblouse	√	√		
Drop waist (slight)			√	√
Drop waist (hip)	√	√	√[1]	√
Drop waist (thigh)	√	√		√
Flapper	√	√		√
Drop waist (elastic)	√	√		
Empire	√		√	
Blouson	√	√[3]		
Drop blouson	√	√		
Fanny wrap	√	√		√[4]
Thigh wrap	√	√		
Tie front	√	√		√[4]
Cocoon	√	√	√	

[1]If the horizontal line of the drop waist ends above
the widest part of the hip
[2]If the shoulder and neck are not too full or fleshy
[3]If the tummy is not protuberant
[4]If the fanny wrap or tie front is at the high hip

DRESSES (NO WAIST)

	H	O	A	X
Float	√	√	√	
Baby-doll smock			√[1]	
Bib dress	√[2]	√[2]	√	
Tent			√	
Muu-muu	√[2]	√[2]	√	
Sheath	√[2]			√
Princess	√[3]		√	√
Coat dress	√[3]		√[4]	√
Chemise	√	√[3]		√
Shirtwaist chemise	√[3]	√[3]		√
Jumper	√	√	√[4]	√[2]
Slip dress	√			√
Tabard	√	√		
Sweater dress	√	√[5]		√
A-line	√		√	√

[1]Shoulder emphasis is good on an **A**, but this is a very "little girl" dress.
[2]If the shoulder area is not thick or fleshy
[3]Soft fabrics only, so as not to look boxy
[4]Must be A-line through the hip
[5]One size larger than usual to avoid cling

SHORTS

	H	O	A	X
Short short	√[1]	√[1]		√
Shorts	√[1]	√[1]		√
Wide-leg cuffed	√[2]	√[2]	√[3]	√
Tap pant	√[2]	√[2]	√[3]	√
Boxer	√[2]	√		√
Skort	√[2]	√[2]	√	√
Jamaica	√[2]	√[2]		√
Bermuda	√[2]	√[2]		√
Walking short	√[2]			√
Wide-leg Bermuda			√[3]	
Wide-leg walking short	√		√	
Romper				√

[1]If legs are good
[2]With elastic waist
[3]If they end below the biggest part of the thigh

PANTS (NARROW)

	H	O	A	X
Straight leg	√			√
Peg leg	√	√		√
Stirrup	√	√		√
Legging	√	√		
Jean				√
Cropped	√	√		√
Capri	√	√		
Knicker	√			√
Toreador	√	√		√
Pedal pusher	√	√		√
Hip yoke	√	√	√	√

PANTS (FULL)

	H	O	A	X
Short culotte	√			√
Culotte	√		√	√
Clam digger	√			√
Pleated trousers	√		√	√
Bell bottom				√
Palazzo		√		
Harem		√		√
Jodhpur		√		√
Jumpsuit	√		√	√
Overall	√	√		

Note: All **H** and **O** pants should have elastic in the waist.

SKIRTS (NARROW)

	H	O	A	X
Straight	√[1]	√[1]		√
Pegged/Hobble	√	√		√
Inverted pleat	√[2]	√[2]		√
Kick pleat	√[1]	√[1]		√
Wrap	√[1]		√[2]	√
Inset pleat	√	√		√
Side pleat	√		√	√
Godet	√[3]	√[3]		√
Trumpet	√[3]	√[3]		√
A-line	√		√	√
Jean skirt	√		√	√
Side slit	√	√[3]		
Slit	√[1]	√[3]		
Modified dirndl	√	√	√	√
Tube	√[4]	√[4]		
Gaucho	√	√	√	√
Split	√[5]		√	√
Golf	√	√	√	√
Hipster				√[6]

[1]If it doesn't "hike" or "ride" on the high hip
[2]Only an A-line wrap
[3]Wonderful on narrow thighs—must have elastic waist
[4]With an overblouse or over sweater
[5]Best in soft fabrics so as not to be boxy
[6]A very young look for young women only

SKIRTS (FULL)

	H	O	A	X
Box pleat			√[1]	√
Knife pleat	√		√	√
Crystal pleat	√	√	√	√
Kilt			√[1]	√
Gored	√[2]		√	√
High waist			√	√
Flared/Semicircle			√	√
Gathered			√	√
Border print	√	√	√	√
Hip yoke	√[2]	√[3]	√[4]	√
Circle			√	√
Peasant			√	√
Bubble			√[5]	√[5]
Bell			√[5]	√[5]
Tiered			√	√
Handkerchief	√		√	√

[1]If stitching of pleat ends well above the wide part of the hipline
[2]If there is elastic in the waist
[3]Same as [2], but with an overblouse
[4]If the yoke ends above the widest part of the hip
[5]A very young look for young women only

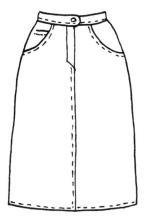

TOPS (BLOUSES AND SHIRTS)

	H	O	A	X
Bow	√		√	√
Ruffled front		√	√	
Poet/Victorian	√		√	√
Cossack			√	√
Surplice			√	√
Peasant	√[1]		√	
Blouson	√	√		
Notched/Convertible collar	√	√[2]	√	√
Collarless front button	√	√[2]	√	√
Fanny wrap	√	√		
Sailor	√[3]	√[3]	√	
Hip-yoke blouson	√	√		
Sport	√	√	√	√
Polo			√	√
Button-down	√	√[2]	√	√
Camp	√		√	√
Lumberjack			√	√
Collarband	√		√	√

[1]If shoulders are not very fleshy
[2]If upper torso is very heavy, softer blouses are preferable.
[3]Best worn as middy overblouse

TOPS (MISCELLANEOUS)

	H	O	A	X
Tank	√			√
Halter				√
Camisole	√			√
Sweatshirt	√	√	√	
Overblouse	√	√		√
T-shirt	√		√	√

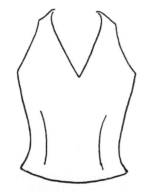

TOPS (SWEATERS)

	H	O	A	X
Cardigan	√	√[1]	√[1]	√
V-neck cardigan	√	√[2]		√
Pullover	√		√	√
Crew	√		√	√
Shell	√		√	√
Skimp	√	√		
Poor boy				√
Turtleneck			√[3]	√
Cowl	√	√	√	√
Tunic	√	√		
Sweater vest	√		√	√
Fisherman			√	√

[1]Unbuttoned
[2]Must be loose—oversized works well
[3]With shoulder pads

COATS

	H	O	A	X
Swagger			√	√
Cape	√	√	√	√
Sherlock Holmes cape	√	√	√	√
Balmacan			√	√
Smock	√	√	√	
Fling	√	√	√	√
Fitted	√			
Princess			√	√
Trench	√		√	√
Redingote			√	√
Chesterfield	√	√		√
Quilted	√[1]			√
Shawl	√			√
Wrap	√			√
Polo/Overcoat	√	√		√
Reefer	√			√
Slicker	√	√		√
Duster	√	√	√	√

[1]Not on a very short body

JACKETS

	H	O	A	X
Blazer	✓		✓	✓
Pea	✓	✓	✓[1]	✓
Topper	✓	✓	✓[1]	✓
Car coat	✓	✓	✓[1]	✓
Eton	✓			✓
Spencer	✓		✓	✓
Wing-back		✓		
Tuxedo	✓			
Norfolk	✓		✓	✓
Safari	✓		✓	✓
Peplum			✓	✓
Fly-away	✓	✓	✓	
Semifitted	✓	✓[2]	✓	✓
Stroller	✓	✓		✓
Parka	✓	✓	✓[1]	✓
Battle jacket	✓	✓		✓
Bolero			✓	✓
Mao	✓	✓		✓
Nehru	✓			✓

[1]If it ends below the widest part of the hip and fits with ease over the hip and thigh area
[2]Unbuttoned if very busty

VESTS

	H	O	A	X
Sweater vest	✓		✓	✓
Tabard	✓	✓		
Maude	✓	✓	✓	
Waist coat			✓	✓
Bolero vest			✓	✓

COLLARS AND NECKLINES (HIGH EMPHASIS)

	H	O	A	X
Convertible	✓	✓	✓	✓
Button-down	✓	✓	✓	✓
Johnny	✓		✓	✓
Winged			✓	✓
Bermuda			✓	✓
Collarband	✓		✓	✓
Peter Pan	✓	✓	✓	✓
Crew	✓	✓	✓	✓
Jewel	✓		✓	✓
Halter				✓
Turtle			✓	✓
Mandarin			✓	✓
Nehru			✓	✓
Cossack			✓	✓
Bertha			✓	✓
Pierrot			✓	✓
Bib			✓	✓
Ruffle			✓	✓
Victorian			✓	✓
Drawstring	✓		✓	✓
Jabot	✓		✓	✓
Bow	✓		✓	✓
Batteau	✓		✓	✓

COLLARS AND NECKLINES (LOW EMPHASIS)

	H	O	A	X
V-neck	√	√		√
Teardrop			√	√
Square			√	√
Sweetheart	√		√	√
Halter vee				√
Décolleté	√	√	√	
Keyhole	√			√
Camisole	√			√
Asymmetric	√		√	√
Off-shoulder			√	√
Scoop		√		
Notched	√	√	√	√
Chelsea	√	√		√
Shawl	√	√	√	√
Portrait	√	√	√	√
Sailor	√	√	√	√
Cowl	√	√	√	√
Drape			√	√
Grecian	√		√	√
Tuxedo	√	√	√	√
Strapless			√	√

SLEEVES

	H	O	A	X
Sleeveless		√	√[1]	
Cap	√	√	√	√
Drop	√	√	√	√
Short	√		√	√
Baby doll			√	√
Puff			√	√
Flutter	√	√	√	√
Carmen Miranda			√	√
Cape	√	√	√	√
Halter				√
Tulip	√	√	√	√
Bell	√	√	√	√
Angel	√	√		√
Dolman	√	√	√	√
Batwing	√[2]	√[2]	√[3]	√[3]
Poet	√	√		√
Bishop			√	√
Ruffled	√	√	√	√
Pleated puff	√		√	√
Gibson			√	√
Raglan	√[4]			√
Long fitted	√	√		√
Seven-eighths	√	√	√	√
Three-quarters			√	√
Elbow			√	√
Minimal	√		√	√
Shirtsleeve	√	√	√	√
French cuff	√	√		√

[1]If upper arms aren't too full
[2]If the waist of the garment is not defined
[3]If the waist of the garment is defined
[4]If the shoulder is padded

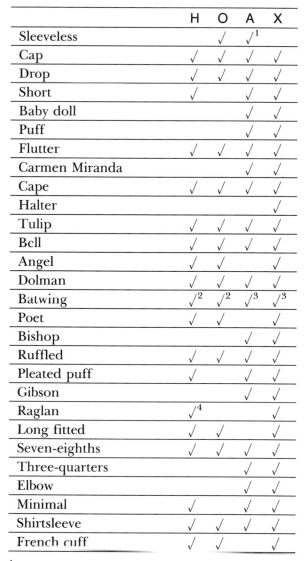

LINGERIE (FOUNDATIONS)

	H	O	A	X
Body briefer	√	√	√[1]	√
Merry widow	√	√	√	√
Waist cincher	√	√		
Control brief	√	√		√
Panty girdle				√
Thigh panty girdle			√	√
Capri girdle			√	
Boned girdle			√[2]	
Corselette	√[2]	√[2]	√[2]	
Soft-cup bra	√		√	
Underwire bra	√	√	√	√
Strapless bra			√	√
Longline bra	√	√		
Longline strapless bra	√	√		
Contour bra	√		√	
Sport bra	√		√	√
Push-up bra (plunge or demi)	√		√	√
Convertible bra	√		√	√

LINGERIE (DAYWEAR)

	H	O	A	X
Full slip	√	√	√	√
Half slip	√	√	√	√
Split petticoat	√	√	√	√
Petticoat			√	√
Camisole	√	√	√	√
Teddy	√	√	√	√
Bikini				√[3]
Brief	√	√	√	√
Tap pant	√	√	√	√
T-shirt			√	√
Shoulder pad	√	√	√	√
Hipster			√	√

[1]If it is loose in the leg band
[2]An old-fashioned and unattractive garment
[3]If the hipline is not very fleshy

LINGERIE (AT HOME AND SLEEPWEAR)

	H	O	A	X
Baby doll	√	√		√
Shorty pajama	√	√		√
Sleepshirt	√	√		√
Oversize T-shirt	√	√		√
Pajama	√			√
Empire gown	√		√	√
Granny gown	√	√	√	√
Caftan	√	√	√	
Illusion caftan	√	√	√	√
Hostess coat	√	√	√	√
Bathrobe			√	√
Housecoat	√	√	√	
Kimono	√		√	√
Robe	√	√	√	
Peignoir & negligee	√	√	√	√

SWIMWEAR

	H	O	A	X
2-piece			√	√
Bikini			√	√
Maillot	√	√	√	√
Surplice			√	√
Boy leg	√	√		
Strapless	√		√	√
Blouson	√	√		
French cut	√	√	√	√
Dressmaker			√	
Tank	√	√		√
Halter	√			√
V-neck	√	√	√	√
Jewel neck				√
Sarong	√	√	√	
Gathered	√	√	√	√
Set-in skirt			√	√
Strapless maillot	√	√	√	

8

Defining Your Own Style

STYLE IS BEST DEFINED as having a sense of what is unique about you and knowing how to project that uniqueness to the world. Before you can do this, you must clearly identify the elements that define your personality—your likes, your dislikes, your moods—and understand how these elements function in the context of your lifestyle. To help you see the total picture, fill out the questionnaires on lifestyle and personality that follow. Then we will discuss the individual styles from which you can choose based on your questionnaire results.

LIFESTYLE QUESTIONNAIRE

1. What do you do for work (including homemaker, volunteer work or school)?

   _____

   _____

   _____

   _____

2. What do you do in your free time (including at home, TV, sports, shopping, etc.)?

   _____

   _____

   _____

   _____

3. What types of dress-up occasions do you have in your life?

   _____

   _____

   _____

   _____

4. Approximately what percentage of your time is spent:

   At work? _____

   At leisure? _____

   At dress up? _____

5. What percentage of your wardrobe dollars would you ideally spend on:

   Work clothes? _____

   Casual clothes? _____

   Dressy clothes? _____

6. Take a quick survey of your closet and list what percentage of clothing you have versus what you need for the following:

	Have	*Need*
Work	_____	_____
Casual	_____	_____
Dressy	_____	_____

PERSONALITY QUESTIONNAIRE

1. List five of your traits that you consider unique or special:

   _____

   _____

   _____

   _____

   _____

2. List ten things you like about yourself and ten you don't like:

Like   *Don't Like*

_____   _____

_____   _____

_____   _____

_____   _____

_____   _____

_____   _____

_____   _____

_____   _____

_____   _____

_____   _____

3. List five accomplishments of which you are particularly proud:

_____

_____

_____

_____

_____

4. Number in order the six most important priorities in your life:

_____	Family	_____	Health
_____	Friends	_____	Appearance
_____	Animals	_____	Peace of mind
_____	Home	_____	Aesthetics
_____	Church	_____	Ethics/Morality
_____	Career	_____	Accomplishment
_____	Civic work	_____	Pleasure
_____	Love/Romance	_____	Power
_____	Intellect	_____	Other
_____	Justice	_____	Other

5. Life Pie

In the mid 1970s I had the opportunity to participate in several training programs given by the Boston Junior League. One exercise that was used regularly was the *Life Pie*. Picture your time as a circle (pie). Divide it into three sections (wedges) representing the percentage of time you spend on:

R = Relationships: family, friends
L = Lifework: career, homemaking, volunteer work
I = Individual interests/spirit: reading, church, meditation, hobbies, grooming (these are the things you do for you).

Frequently, it is necessary to be out of balance (equal parts) because of one's role or stage of life. A mother with small children or a lawyer climbing the firm's ladder, for example, may find that relationships or lifework are occupying 70% of their waking hours. The goal, however, is to achieve a balance between these three areas, and temporary imbalances should not be allowed to become permanent. We need time and energy for each of these vitally important areas of life.

Draw a life pie and repeat it whenever you find yourself out of sorts, bored or burned-out. It might provide the answer to what is wrong and a possible clue to the solution.

This is how my life pie looked while I was writing this book:

THE LIFE PIE
R = Relationships
L = Lifework
I = Individual

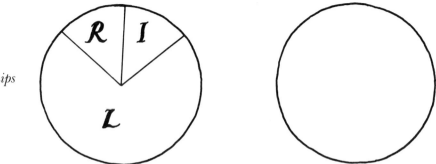

Fill out the one at right for yourself. Is your life in balance?

Classic on Liliana: *One of the most ladylike looks and women's first choice in styles.*
COURTESY JEFF FLAX

Romantic on Colleen: *The most enduring style because it is ageless and works on all body-types.*
COURTESY HEDREN

STYLE CHOICES

Women make a terrible fashion mistake when their external images do not coincide with their internal values, priorities and lifestyles. Clothing, accessories, hair and makeup are aids that we use to tell the world about us as individuals, and style is the medium by which we make our statements. Following is a description of the major styles of dress available to us, each with its own distinct look. Review the style categories and circle those that you like:

THE TRADITIONALS

Classic: Conservative and traditional (Grace Kelly, Dina Merrill, Lauren Bacall, Shari Belafonte-Harper), her clothes are simple but rarely overdone, and she radiates poise and cool confidence in her dress and demeanor. She is never outlandish; others see her as non-controversial. Classic works on everyone.

Romantic: Soft and feminine (Jane Seymour, Princess Diana, Donna Mills, almost all beauty-pageant winners), her clothes are delicate in line, color and texture but rarely overdone. She is never man-tailored. Others see her as gentle. Romantic works best on soft, round or large bodies and is good on both mature and young women. Very young Romantics can "do" ingenue.

Preppy/Tweedy: Extremely simple and durable (Ali McGraw, Cheryl Tiegs, Kate Jackson, Sarah Ferguson), her clothes are expensive and uniform (she wears pink and green a lot) and she is never "glitzy." Others see her as upper-middle class, unimaginative and possibly snobbish. Preppy/Tweedy looks best on tall, young, slender bodies. Because it lacks imagination and is excessively safe, I like to see women beyond college age grow away from Preppy/Tweedy as their primary style choice.

Sporty/Casual: Easy and comfortable (Katharine Hepburn, Farrah Fawcett, Chris Evert-Lloyd), her clothes are relaxed and suitable for the active life. She is never contrived, and others see her as healthy, non-pretentious and relaxed. Sporty/Casual works best on straight figures (H, O) and on women whose lifestyles

Preppy/Tweedy *on Karen: Best on young women.*
COURTESY ROYAL WOMAN

Sporty/Casual *on Meg: Popular with most women because of its ease and versatility.*
COURTESY JEFF FLAX

Elegant *on Colleen: Calls for simplicity, perfectionistic attention to details, and a quest for quality.*
COURTESY HEDREN

and personalities indicate a preference for "au natural."

Elegant: Formal and perfect in simplicity (Nancy Reagan, Catherine Deneuve, Audrey Hepburn), her clothes are studied and show incredible flair and attention to detail. She is never thrown together. Others see her as aloof, well-bred and assured. Elegant works on any woman who has the time, money and energy for its perfectionist standards.

Career/Executive: Professional and no-nonsense (Diane Sawyer, Jane Wyman, Barbara Walters, Sandra Day O'Connor), her clothes are subtle and designed to be secondary to her work function. She is never fussy or flashy. Others see her as serious and responsible, if a bit unfeminine (although new career looks are softer and prettier). Career/Executive works on all women except the **X** who is too curvy for many of the Career/Executive straight lines. The **X** must choose soft, slightly curved looks to carry off Career/Executive.

Natural Fiber: Simple and refined (Jane Fonda, Dinah Shore, Candace Bergen), her clothes are silk, linen,

cotton and wool, and tend toward solid colors. She is never wash-and-wear and doesn't care about the wrinkles of many natural fabrics. Others see her as cool and more concerned with quality than with quantity. Natural Fiber works best on medium and slim figures, as fabrics that wrinkle (silk, linen) or are stiffer and buckle (cotton, wool) can make a large woman look messy or wide.

THE BOLDS

Glamorous: Done up to the nines and sparkling (Elizabeth Taylor, Bernadette Peters, Joan Collins), her clothes are sexy and a bit overdone. Not that she cares—the more cleavage, feathers, flash and glitter, the better! Others see her as dangerously female. She is never sleek and simple if she can help it. Glamorous looks best on curvy figures (A, X) and on some busty O figures, but is generally not good on mature women (Liz? Joan?) or on those lacking the confidence to withstand stares.

Career/Executive on Jeannie: Looks for the working woman have expanded from the "cookie-cutter" suit and bow tie to softer separate looks, knits and dresses.
COURTESY ROYAL WOMAN

Natural Fiber on Jodi: Understated and works best for thin or medium-sized women.
COURTESY JEFF FLAX

Glamorous on Jodi: Best on curvy figures.
COURTESY JEFF FLAX

Artsy/Radical Chic on Jeannie: *Requires immense self-knowledge and imagination.*

Belle/Femme Fatale on Gabrielle: *The woman who dresses for men—sometimes overdoing it!*

Artsy/Radical Chic: Unusual and imaginative (Angelica Huston, Tina Turner, Natalia Makarova), her clothes range from thrift store to one-of-a-kind designer boutique items, all put together with a flair that is all her own. She is a trend-setter and is never one for anything obvious (matched suits or coordinated separates). Others see her as liberal, artistic and original. Artsy/Radical Chic works best on slim or average-sized, medium height or tall women who have natural drama and the restraint not to dress like a leftover love child (Woodstock is over!).

Belle/Femme Fatale: Flouncy feminine or very, very female (Barbara Cartland, Zsa-Zsa/Eva Gabor, Dolly Parton, Audrey Landers), her clothes run the gamut from baby-doll cute to frou-frou or blatantly sexy. She is never given to tailored looks and feels sorry for women who are. Others see her as fluttery feminine or as sexy in an obvious way. Belle/Femme Fatale are two styles, but they are often worn by the same woman because their intents are the same—to please men. Belle is too fussy to work on any but young, slim figures, while Femme Fatale works only on curvy figures and is hard to carry off. Women over 35 risk coming off as mutton dressed as lamb in either style. However, Belle/Femme Fatale can be fun as an occasional at-home look with that special someone.

Western: Studded and denim (Barbara Mandrell, Loretta Lynn, Minnie Pearl—"How-dee!"), her clothes are totally inspired by regional tradition and range (as in "Home on the . . .") from jeans to Annie Oakley to *Hee Haw*. She owns two pair of shoes, cowboy boots and 4-inch heels. She is horrified by city-slicker sophisticated looks, and like the Belle, is charmed by "cute." Others see her as comfortable and full of homey country common sense. Classic good taste (whatever that is) is not her thing. Western works best on slim and average Hs and curvy (A, X) bodies, and is generally silly on women over 35 (except, of course, Minnie—she's an original).

Dramatic: Elegant and show-stopping (Princess Stephanie, Bianca Jagger, Paloma Picasso), her clothes are painstakingly put together to achieve maximum

Dramatic *on Virginia: Bold and startling looks for great entrances and envious stares. Not all women can wear Dramatic.*

COURTESY JEFF FLAX

Western *on Martha: Denim—even when studded, beaded or embroidered—denotes young and casual.*

COURTESY POLSKY

effect when she enters a room and all eyes turn. She is never given to ruffles or soft classic dressing, but rather chooses severe lines and startling accessories. Others see her as showy and very confident. Dramatic works best on women who are tall and very straight (H) and on some who are very curvy (A, X). The O is usually done in by high drama.

Man-tailored/Machisma: Masculine and pared down (Grace Jones, Diane Keaton á la Annie Hall), her clothes are starkly mannish, often in contrast to her high drama (Grace) or to her inescapable cuteness (Diane). She is

Man-tailored/Machisma on Mary: Must be countered by softness in makeup lest it be too severe.
COURTESY DENNIS BUTLER

Trendy on Karla: For those who are up-to-the-minute with fashion.
COURTESY JEFF FLAX

never one for fussy femme fatale looks. Others see her as offbeat and original, if a bit androgynous. Man-tailored/Machisma works on all body types, and is best if the wearer knows how to use feminine hair and makeup to balance the look so it doesn't look "butch."

Trendy: Up-to-the-minute, fashionable and even avant garde (Cher, Madonna), her clothes emphasize her interest in what's going on now and can be an expensive habit as fads come and go. She never cares whether an item will look good in 5 years as she will replace it in 5 months (or less) with the latest. Others see her as a "with it" clothes horse and a bit of a follower who is impressed with what the "in" crowd is doing. Trendy works on all body types. It is best for those who are not compulsive about it, but blend trendy with more durable wardrobe purchases. Adding a few trendy accessories or garments each year can be an easy, fun way to update your wardrobe.

NAMING YOUR STYLES

As our moods and roles change, so does our style. Recently I read a book that attempted to classify all styles of dressing into a handful of categories and said that a woman was only to dress in one of these styles. I found this theory limiting. I dress by style according to my role, my mood, or for a desired effect, as shown by the following examples:

Role	*Style*
Commentating fashion shows	Elegant/Classic
Going to New York collections	Elegant
Dating	Romantic
Shopping	Classic/Casual
Working in office	Casual/Classic
At home	Casual/Romantic

In short, I am an elegant, classic, romantic, casual type! Clearly they cannot all happen at once (no one can "do" Grace Kelly and Dolly Parton at the same time). Knowing your best style looks (plural) and their applicability to your various roles is the key to dressing well. Your wardrobe can then be built, or rebuilt, in proportion to your lifestyle needs and unique personality, with only your body type as a constant.

Review the styles you have checked off and list your first choice and three optional choices:

Style: First choice

_____

Style: Optional choices

_____

_____

_____

Classic

Romantic

Preppy/Tweedy

Review your Lifestyle Questionnaire and Personality Questionnaire and consider whether your style choices reflect your clothing needs and personality.

Style (e.g., Romantic)	*Lifestyle Applicability (Work, Dress-up, Home)*	*Projected Personality Traits (Soft, Feminine, Confident)*
1. _____	_____	_____
	_____	_____
	_____	_____
2. _____	_____	_____
	_____	_____
	_____	_____
3. _____	_____	_____
	_____	_____
	_____	_____
4. _____	_____	_____
	_____	_____
	_____	_____

If you feel that any of your chosen styles does not work with your lifestyle and personality, choose another.

Sporty/Casual

Elegant

Career/Executive

Natural Fiber

Glamorous

Artsy/Radical Chic

Belle/Femme Fatale

Western

Dramatic

Man-tailored/Machisma

Trendy

Many women choose classic or sporty alone and are afraid to try other styles. While I feel that a woman is predominantly Traditional or Bold, it makes for a more interesting wardrobe to have more than one or two looks.

Many women over 40 fear dressing too young and appearing foolish. In general, I like to see all women of voting age dress as grown-up women (European women do—American women frequently don't). There is a big difference between grown-up lady clothes and old lady clothes. All women can and should wear grown-up lady clothes and look wonderful. After all, we earn our years and adulthood is its own reward!

STYLE IS . . .

- Knowing yourself.
- Projecting that knowledge in dress, grooming, carriage, entertainment and home.
- Developing a sense of good taste.
- Not looking like everybody else.
- Getting organized.
- Taking time to be selective.
- Paying attention to details.
- Caring enough about yourself to do all of the above.

Style is something that can be developed. It is not dependent on:

- Natural beauty
- Age
- Slimness
- Money

Style is right up there with *confidence* and *charm* as something that counts!

9

Shaping Your Body with Color, Texture and Line

Maureen is using color, texture, line, form (and a great hat) to balance an A figure.

COURTESY ROYAL WOMAN

AFTER A FASHION SHOW in Dayton, Ohio, a woman suggested that I explain a little theory of visual design in my book. All things visual come down to four basic elements:

- Color
- Texture
- Line and form

Believing that these four elements can be used to balance the figure, I have developed *The Theory of Visual* H-O-A-X!

COLOR

There are three aspects to any color: hue, intensity and value. Once you understand these, you can learn to use them in dressing to visually give your figure the proportions you want.

Hue is the actual name of a color as it exists on the color wheel. Let's take red as our example.

Value is the darkness or lightness of a color, which is determined by how much white or black has been added to it. *Tint* is the addition of white. Add white to red and you get pink, which is a tint of red. *Shade* is the addition of black. Add black to red and you get maroon, which is a shade of red.

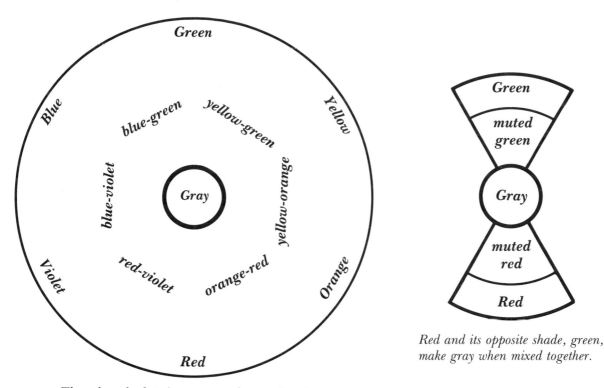

The color wheel: primary, secondary and tertiary hues

Red and its opposite shade, green, make gray when mixed together.

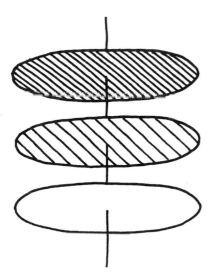

Tints and shades of a hue are made by adding white or black.

Intensity is the clarity of a color, which is determined by how much of its opposite color has been added. When two colors that are opposite on the color wheel are mixed, you get gray (e.g., red + green = gray). If you add a little green to true red you get a grayed, muted red—a less *intense* red, or "soft red."

WHAT COLORS MEAN TO US

Color is very emotional; it has the power to move and to change moods. Think of the colors of:

- the sea
- the sun
- the mountains
- the forest
- the atmosphere
- the garden

- Arizona
- autumn
- jewels
- night
- balloons

Our psychological appreciation of color has to do with the many perceptions of our lives. For example, one woman may see red as the color of blood dating back to a bloody skinned knee in her childhood, while another sees red as positive and energetic dating back to her first balloon or a little red wagon. Such associations are called *connotations.* Some common color connotations are:

White: Clean, pure, young, joyful—or blank, colorless.

Black: Sophisticated, expensive, severe, mysterious, stark, simple—or mournful, glum, depressing, sneaky.

Red: Passionate, positive, optimistic, happy, sexy—or angry, sinful, competitive, bellicose.

Blue: Cool, quiet, restful, peaceful—or lonely, sad, cold, depressed.

Green: Energetic, lively, successful, growing, springlike, calm—or greedy, overactive, envious.

Yellow: Sunny, optimistic, active, cheerful, wealthy, wise—or cowardly, gaudy, sick.

Purple: Regal, rich, powerful, passionate, mature—or flashy, old, sad, tired, bruised.

Orange: Fresh, fruity, happy, modern, unique—or flashy, bold, obvious, hot.

Gray: Mature, dignified, strong, subtle, restful—or dull, gloomy, cold, boring, old.

Brown: Homey, earthy, secure, warm, safe—or boring, rusty, dark, ordinary, dirty.

Fuchsia: Sexy, passionate, womanly—or blatant, flashy, restless, untrustworthy.

Beige: Subtle, earthy, true, natural, expensive—or colorless, dingy, dull, ordinary.

CHOOSING YOUR *COLORS*

In the early 1980s when seasonal color analysis became the rage, I was the first on my block to become a devotee—perhaps to the extreme. I'm a Winter who over the past few years has strayed from the path of color truth, however, into the land of off-white, hot gold, peach, seafoam and tomato soup red. Further, I have the nerve to look nice in these colors!

One day a friend mimicked me, saying: "I'm a July 3 with a little November 8th myself."

Many women have loved seasonal color theory, while others have taken a dim view of its limiting choices or confusing descriptions. Whichever is the case for you, I suggest a new approach to color:

- Understand its potential.
- Review what you like emotionally.
- Identify the colors that seem to complement you.
- Choose 10 or 15 colors with which to build a core wardrobe that is pared down in colors and therefore easier to plan and accessorize.

I wear about 15 colors—maximum—and it makes my shopping easier because my eye zooms in on these shades and my closet looks homogeneous. Here are my current wardrobe colors:

Winter Wardrobe	Summer Wardrobe	Both	This Year
Winter white	Yellow	White	Hot gold
Royal blue	Pink	Black	
Purple	Seafoam	Hot turquoise	
Kelly green		Red	
Pale gray		Peach	
		Hot pink	

Picking the colors you wear requires some thought, but it is well worth the effort. The trick is to separate the colors you wear from the colors you merely like. For example, I like olive green but look half-dead in it; I look good in navy but don't like it. I wear neither. Consider the following points in analyzing *your* color choices.

- Colors you like reflect your experiences with colors—your color connotations.

- The colors you wear reflect what you think about yourself and are trying to project to the rest of the world. For example, the brunette woman who wants to stand out at a party might wear hot pink while the shy blonde woman wishing to blend in might wear beige, or the gray-haired woman wishing to be taken seriously in the corporate world might wear gray or navy.

Take this analysis a step further with the H-O-A-X Color Chart, which will help you pinpoint the colors around which you want to build your wardrobe.

THE H-O-A-X *COLOR CHART*

1. Put a letter (L) by the colors you like most and a (W) by the colors you wear well:

Cool Subdued Tones	*Warm Subdued Tones*
Black	Medium or dark brown
Navy	Dark olive
Maroon	Burgundy
Charcoal gray or Slate	Taupe
Dark brown	Rust
Forest green	Teal blue
Purple	Deep mustard

Cool Vibrant Tones	*Warm Vibrant Tones*
Lemon yellow	Gold or Bright yellow
Clear red	Orange
Fuchsia or Hot pink	Tomato soup red
Turquoise	Hot aqua
Royal blue	Periwinkle
White	Cream or Winter white
Clear green	Lime green

Cool Pastel Tones	*Warm Pastel Tones*
Pale pink	Peach or Coral
Mauve	Lavender
Pale blue	Baby blue
Ice green	Muted jade
Pale seafoam	Olive green
Ice yellow	Mustard or Camel
Pale gray	Beige

2. The largest number of colors I wear are in the cool/warm category (circle one) and in the subdued/vibrant/pastel subcategory (circle one). The colors I wear well are (try to limit to twelve):

_____   _____

_____   _____

_____   _____

_____   _____

_____   _____

_____   _____

3. Some colors I like in general, but which don't look good on me are:

_____   _____

_____   _____

_____   _____

USING COLOR TO REBALANCE YOUR FIGURE

Now that you have narrowed your wardrobe color choices, you can begin to use your chosen colors to "recontour" your shape. A few tips make this a simple process.

Light and bright (pastel and vibrant) colors visually "come forward," thus emphasizing or enlarging.

Dark and muted (subdued) colors visually "recede" in the eye, thus de-emphasizing or minimizing.

Contrasting colors can be used cleverly in separates to alter a woman's appearance of overall height, width and figure shape. Contrasting colors can be sharply different colors or extremes of light and dark:

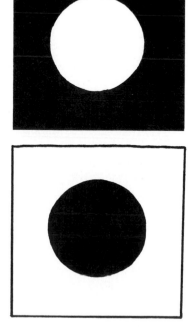

White comes forward and looks larger, while black recedes.

• **Total extremes** (e.g., black and white) tend to shorten a figure by dividing it into distinct sections. Care must be taken not to let the two segments be exactly even in length as the proportion will appear square and wide. The darker section of the figure, however will appear narrower, and the lighter portion will appear wider.

For the **A** *or* **X***, a dark skirt and light top are best. (Note spectators with dark stockings—smashing!)*

For the **H** *and* **O***, a light bottom and dark top are best.*

COURTESY ROYAL WOMAN

- **Tint and shade** of the same hue (e.g., pink and cranberry) have an effect similar to total extremes. However, tint and shade color contrasts are more subtle, and the common hue gives them less of a shortening effect.
- **Bright, high-intensity** colors used in separate dressing (e.g., red and green) tend to color block the body into two wider, shorter segments.
- **Monochromatic dressing** refers to clothing and accessories that are the same color from top to bottom (e.g., pale pink shirt, slacks, hose and shoes). Monochromatic dressing slims and elongates the figure, and for that reason it is used by many movie and TV stars.

Monotone dressing works on all body types.

- **Different hues of similar values** (e.g., pale pink and winter white or deep royal and black) have almost the same effect as monochromatic dressing.

CONTRAST	H	O	A	X
Dark top/light or bright bottom	√	√		√
Light or bright top/dark bottom	√		√	√
Pastel top/pastel bottom	√	√	√	√
Dark top/dark bottom	√	√	√	√
Bright top/bright bottom	√*	√*	√*	√*
Monochromatic top/bottom	√	√	√	√

Note: Top may include scarves, necklaces and earrings, and bottom may include hose and shoes.

*Don't attempt this unless your height is average or tall and you are very confident. Bright contrasting separates tend to color-block the body into two wide rectangles.

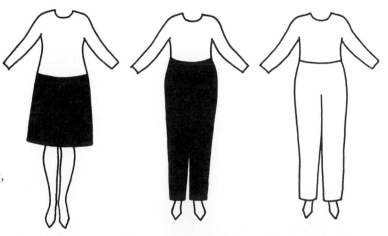

Contrast versus monotone dressing. In contrast, balance is the issue.

TEXTURE

Texture is feel. It is also reflection of light and weight. These elements are further broken down this way:

- *Feel:* smooth, rough, soft, hard
- *Light:* shine, semigloss, matte
- *Weight:* thick, medium, light

The feel, light reflection and weight of a garment affect the way it drapes on the body and the way it is perceived by the eye. The most minimizing textures are *smooth, soft, matte* and *lightweight.* The most maximizing textures are *rough, hard, shiny and thick.*

Imagine a woman of medium height who wears size 16. Picture her at two parties in two outfits. The first is a georgette blouse and wool crepe pants, the second is a heavy satin blouse and blanket-wool pants. Clearly, the first outfit is more flattering.

You can use texture to balance your figure if you use light, soft, matte textures to de-emphasize, and avoid rough, thick, shiny fabrics anywhere that your body is particularly full. For example, I have a big midriff but I love the fabric charmeuse (light, soft, but shiny). I also love sweater knits (thick, rough and matte). I compromise by not wearing charmeuse at my midriff (no camisoles), but I do wear charmeuse for party pajamas, pants, shirts, and blouson blouses with padded shoulders and long pearls that distract. The only sweater knits I wear are those which are padded in the shoulder and oversized enough to miss my midriff entirely.

Texture can vary within the body of a garmet with the use of details and trims. *Details* are pleats, smocking, tucks and seam stitching. *Trims* are braid, beads, applique, embroidery, ribbons, buttons, bows, etc.

The following Texture Chart will clarify which textures flatter each H-O-A-X body type. This will show you how to use texture in a way similar to color to balance your figure.

TEXTURE CHART

T = Top
B = Bottom

Next to each texture definition are impressions associated with fabrics of that texture.

	H		O		A		X	
	T	B	T	B	T	B	T	B
TEXTURE FEEL								
Rough (modern, earthy, natural)	√		√		√			√
Hard (formal, protected, severe)	√	√			√	√	√	
Smooth (simple, cool, elegant)	√	√	√	√	√	√	√	√
Soft (feminine, romantic, sensual)	√	√	√	√	√	√	√	√
TEXTURE WEIGHT								
Thick (adds volume)					√			
Medium (changes little)	√		√		√	√	√	√
Light (slims and drapes)	√	√	√	√	√	√	√	√
TEXTURE LIGHT REFLECTION								
Shiny (bright, confident, female)	√	√	√*	√	√			√
Semigloss (warm, crisp, fresh)	√	√	√*	√	√		√	√
Matte (cool, sure, sophisticated)	√	√	√	√	√	√	√	√

*Only charmeuse and lightweight glossy fabrics that are worn as dressy blouses, blousoned over the bottom.

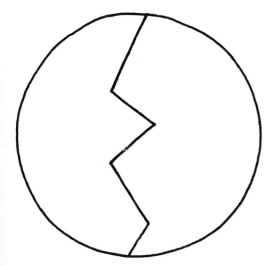

Form (the circle) and line (the zig-zag)

LINE AND FORM

For the purposes of fashion, form equals silhouette (form = silhouette). Imagine a garment's form as its *outside shape* from any angle and its line as what goes on *within* that shape. You can see this clearly in the illustrations of garments in Chapter 7, The **H-O-A-X** *Glossary of Styles*. The drawings show garment form only, omitting interior details (line). Form is three-dimensional, but line occurs within form, so it is two-dimensional. Line is the two-dimensional space between two points. Line can be:

- Vertical
- Horizontal
- Diagonal
- Curved
- In motion
- Straight

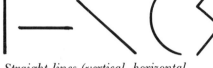

Straight lines (vertical, horizontal, diagonal), a curved line and a line in motion

Line can be thick, as when a belt cuts horizontally across the waist, or thin, as is the side seam of pants. It can also be the major statement of a garment, such as the braid on a Chanel suit, or it can be as subtle as the side seams of a dark dress.

Line, like color and texture, has distinct emotional connotations:

- Vertical (solid, conservative)
- Horizontal (restful, graceful)
- Diagonal (active, sophisticated)
- Curved (feminine, sensual)
- In motion (frantic, modern)
- Straight (severe, unbinding)

Line, more than any other visual element, can serve the H-O-A-X principle of "distract, not disguise."

LINES FOR H-O-A-X BODIES

Picture the four bodies as bottles:

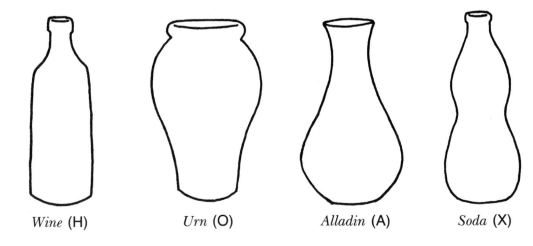

Wine (H)   *Urn (O)*   *Alladin (A)*   *Soda (X)*

(Above) Reversed striping and hip emphasis work on the H *and* O.

COURTESY GRANDE DAME

(Right) Horizontal lines on top, padded shoulders and wide-leg shorts balance the A *figure and also work on the* X.

COURTESY JEFF FLAX

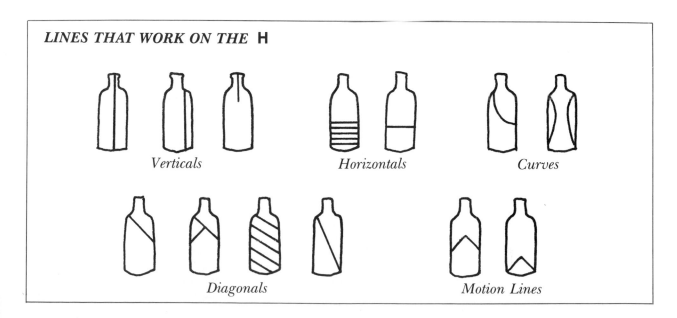

LINES THAT WORK ON THE H

Verticals   *Horizontals*   *Curves*

Diagonals   *Motion Lines*

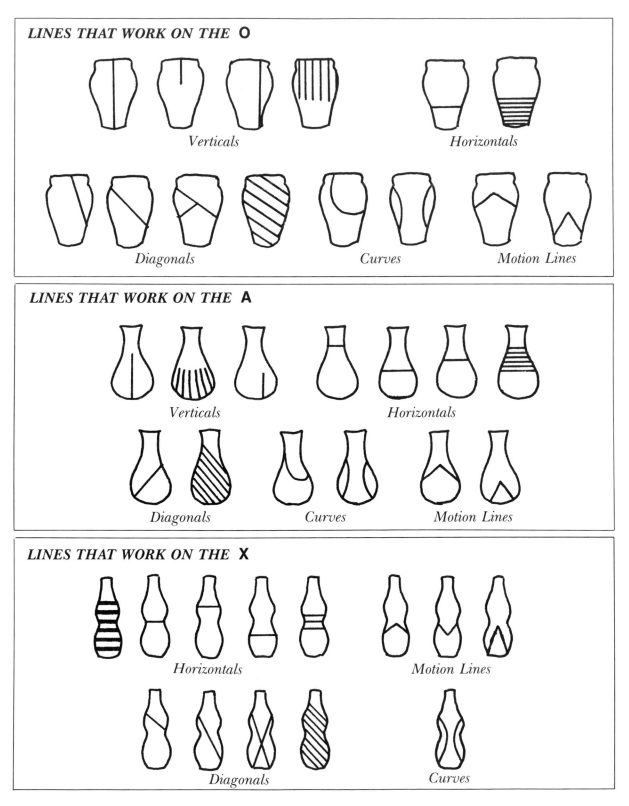

LINES THAT WORK ON THE O

Verticals

Horizontals

Diagonals

Curves

Motion Lines

LINES THAT WORK ON THE A

Verticals

Horizontals

Diagonals

Curves

Motion Lines

LINES THAT WORK ON THE X

Horizontals

Motion Lines

Diagonals

Curves

PUTTING COLOR, TEXTURE AND LINE TOGETHER

Fill out the following information about color, texture and line for *your* body based on what you now know about your shape's best and worst features.

1. My best colors are:

    _____   _____

    _____   _____

    _____   _____

    _____   _____

    _____   _____

    In dressing with separates, where on my body do I put:

    Light and bright colors?   _____

    Dark and muted colors?   _____

2. My best textures are:

    _____   _____

    Where on my body do I wear my best textures?

    _____   _____

    _____   _____

    My worst textures are:

    _____   _____

    Where on my body do I avoid my worst textures?

    _____   _____

    _____   _____

3. My best lines are:

    Verticals at the (part of body):

    _____   _____

    _____   _____

Horizontals at the (part of body):

_____   _____

_____   _____

Diagonals at the (part of body):

_____   _____

_____   _____

Curves at the (part of body):

_____   _____

_____   _____

Motion lines at the (part of body):

_____   _____

_____   _____

Small plaids (or prints) have the same effect as solids.

Large plaids make horizontal and vertical lines of their own as do wide stripes.

Horizontal details only work at a proportionally narrow part of your body.

Small prints work on any body type (Sally is an **X***).*
COURTESY MOORE

PLAIDS, PRINTS AND STRIPES

Plaids, prints and stripes can get confusing when you try to apply the principles of color, texture and line to them. For that reason, we deal with them separately. The following points should answer most questions:

- If the design is small, plaids and prints should be handled as solid-color treatments.
- If the design is large, plaids and prints should be handled the same as bright or light colors.
- Big stripes should be regarded as repeated horizontal, vertical or diagonal lines.
- Neither large plaids, large prints nor wide horizontal stripes should be used where the body is thickest.

PLAIDS, PRINTS AND STRIPES CHART

T = Top
B = Bottom

	H T	H B	O T	O B	A T	A B	X T	X B
Big plaids			√		√			√
Small plaids	√	√	√	√	√	√	√	√
Big prints			√		√			√
Small prints	√	√	√	√	√	√	√	√
Wide horizontal stripes			√		√			√
Narrow horizontal stripes			√		√		√	√
Vertical or diagonal stripes	√	√	√			√	√	√

10

Using Accessories the H-O-A-X *Way*

LIZ DILLON, a very elegant model, says that the aim of fashion is "not to disguise but to distract." This premise is a cornerstone of the H-O-A-X fashion formula, and it is particularly applicable in regard to accessories. Liz and I agree that nothing can move the eye faster than accessories.

In a nutshell, accessories for the four body types should do the following:

H *ACCESSORIES*

- Cut a vertical line down the body.
- Emphasize the legs.
- Take the eye away from the middle.
- Draw attention to the face.

O *ACCESSORIES*

- Cut a vertical line down the upper body.
- De-emphasize the neck and shoulders.
- Emphasize the legs.
- Add height or draw the eye upward.

A *ACCESSORIES*

- Emphasize the waist.
- Broaden or add bulk or emphasis to the upper torso.
- Slim the leg and foot.
- Take the eye away from the hip and thigh.

The hat, earrings and pin rivet your attention on Audrey's lovely face and eyes, illustrating a H-O-A-X *principle: Emphasize good features.*

COURTESY MAMORU

Huge dangle hoops like Jodi's usually work best for A's and X's with long necks (O's and H's often have shorter necks).

X *ACCESSORIES*

- De-emphasize the chest.
- Emphasize the waist.
- Slim the leg and foot.
- Broaden the shoulder.

On the following page is a chart showing which basic accessories flatter each of the **H-O-A-X** body types. Each category of accessories will be discussed in detail later in this chapter. With accessories more than with garments, you must let your eye be your guide. Because accessories are accents with numerous variations on a theme, general rules are more difficult to apply. In judging whether an accessory works with an outfit, remember the general rules (listed above) for your body type. Then ask: "Does this accessory call attention to an area of my body that I want to emphasize or de-emphasize? Does it distract from or accentuate my body features?"

Accessories can create a mood of their own. Meg's gypsy look is all costume jewelry on a simple black dress.
COURTESY JEFF FLAX

The beautiful choker accentuates **X** *Tara's long neck.*
COURTESY JEFF FLAX

ACCESSORIES Á LA H-O-A-X

	H	O	A	X
PEARLS, CHAINS, BEADS				
Choker		√	√	
18-inch-length	√	√	√	√
Opera/Flapper	√	√		
NECKLACES (OTHER)				
Chunky			√	
Long	√	√		
Pendant	√	√	√	√
BRACELETS				
Chunky		√	√	
Delicate	√	√	√	√
Ankle	NO	NO	NO	NO
WATCHES				
Large		√	√	
Delicate	√	√	√	√
EARRINGS				
Small		√	√	
Medium	√	√	√	√
Large		√	√[1]	√
Dangly				√
Hoops	√		√	√
PINS				
Brooch	√		√	√
Pin	√	√	√	√
BELTS (SOFT)				
Sash/Self		√	√	
Leather tie		√	√	
Cummerbund		√	√	
BELTS (HARD)				
Elastic	√	√	√	√
Leather	√		√	√
Cinch			√	√
Link	√		√	√
Stiff fabric-covered	√		√	√
GLOVES				
Wrist	√			√
7-button	√	√	√	√
Elbow	√	√	√	√
Mitten				√
Gauntlet			√	√

	H	O	A	X
SCARVES (SQUARE)				
18-inch			√	√
36-inch			√	√
45-inch	√	√	√	√
SCARVES (OTHER)				
Oblong	√		√	√
Long thin			√	√
Shawl	√	√	√	√
Tie				√
SUNGLASSES	√	√	√	√
SHOULDER PADS	√	√	√	√
HANDBAGS				
Clutch	√	√	√	√
Satchel			√	√
Handles purse	√	√	√	√
Evening	√	√	√	√
Shoulder	√	√		√
Tote	√	√		√
HATS				
Small[2]	√	√		√
Medium	√	√	√	√
Large[3]	√		√	√
HOSIERY AND SOCKS				
Knee-hi's[4] (hosiery or socks)	√	√		√
Pantyhose	√	√	√	√
Garter belt/stockings[5]	√	√	√	√
Control top	√	√	√	√
Support	√	√	√	√
Textured hose	√	√	√[6]	√
Colored hose	√	√	√[6]	√

[1] If the face is very round or square, avoid earrings that stick out a lot.

[2] Veils are for evening only. They look silly with daytime suits.

[3] Wide horizontal lines, like big picture hats, are not for short women.

[4] Never with dresses; they show when you cross your legs, and look goofy!

[5] But only if you have no flesh on your upper hips (I never met such a woman).

[6] Medium and darker colors and small patterns tend to minimize lower body heaviness.

ACCESSORY RULE #1: BUY GOOD ACCESSORIES

Nothing, in my opinion, looks worse or wastes money more than tacky accessories. Buy good accessories a little at a time (on sale, whenever possible). Years ago I bought a black elastic belt with a rhinestone buckle in Paris. It cost $60 and I thought I was being very frivolous. Yet today, that belt is still my prize and has outlived more than $60 worth of disposable junk accessories I could have purchased at bargain rates.

Begin with basics and go for trendy later on. No matter how classic your style, by the way, the trendy accessory of the year—military pins, real silver hoops, long, cheap (they're lighter) pearls—will update your wardrobe and will usually be good for a few seasons. Over a few years you can build a wonderful wardrobe of accessories.

At the height of the gold chain craze in the late 1970s, I decided to give up buying costume jewelry and buy instead one piece of real gold jewelry every 6 months or so with all the money I would have spent on impulse items. By 1980, I had a beautiful collection of gold chains, earrings and bracelets. In the mid 1980s, costume jewelry became fashion's "it." I collected a limited number of wonderful good pieces and still avoided street vendors and $3 nonsense goodies. (In 1985 a certain airline ran over my jewelry and best clothes with *six* luggage trucks, and I lost several key items, but that's another story!)

ACCESSORY RULE #2: THE RULE OF TWO

If you wish to use accessories in a color that is not in the main body of your outfit, use the color at least twice (e.g., yellow gloves and earrings with a black-and-white dress.) The reason for this is because two or more uses of the color build the color as a theme, whereas a single use of color looks out of place, as if your outfit were thrown together without thought. If one of the accesssories is something that you take off, such as gloves, have a third accessory in that color. The Rule of

Novelty gloves and hat in the same color brighten up Karen's outerwear treatment and illustrate the Accessory Rule of Two.

Two works every time and is a wonderful way to make a small emerging wardrobe seem more versatile.

JEWELRY

- Anything that cuts (chunky bracelets or necklaces, ankle chains) shortens and widens.
- Inexpensive costume pearls are wonderful. Years ago I was at a cocktail party wearing two strands of cheap pearls (and a dress, of course), and I heard a man say, "I love a woman in pearls." I keep mine (opera length) on a wooden hanger so they don't tangle.
- Ball or semi-sphere earrings make the face look wider.
- Drop earrings make the short neck look more so.
- Large earrings look good on most large women.
- Artificial (faux) gems in earrings that match the colors (look closely—there are many) in your iris are dazzling.
- Holiday seasons are wonderful for glitz. If something strikes you as unique and clever, grab it! You'll love it. (I have a fat 3-inch ivory cherub pin I wear at Christmas and a pair of 2-inch blue rhinestone half-moon earrings that get raves).

Long beads elongate, making them an excellent accessory for X's and O's.

COURTESY JEFF FLAX

BELTS

- Women with **H** or **O** bodies can wear belts dropped to the hip (about 2 inches).
- Elastic belts must not be uncomfortably tight.
- Short women should not wear belts of contrasting color. This cuts them in half visually, shortening their line.
- Average-height women can wear a contrasting belt but should repeat the color near the neck in the scarf, collar or earrings (Rule of Two).
- Tall women look best in a contrasting belt, but again, the color should be repeated elsewhere in the outfit.
- Short-waisted women should match the belt color to the color in the top of the outfit to elongate the waist. Long-waisted women should match the belt color to the bottom of the outfit to shorten the waist.

SCARVES

The same rules apply to scarves as to jewelry:
- Fussy (as in chunky) scarf treatments around the neck and shoulder are only for the **A** body type.
- Long vertical scarf treatments are best for **H** and **O** types.
- Scarf treatments extending past the nipples are out for the **X** and full-busted **O**'s. The scarf tends to hang off the bust as if it were a shelf, emphasizing the full bust.
- If you wear a lot of prints, collect scarves in your favorite solids.
- If you wear simple clothes and solid colors, look for rich prints in scarves.
- Print scarves work with tweeds, plaids and stripes only if they are in exactly the same color combination.

SCARF TREATMENTS

Men's tie
H, O, A

Long scarf, knotted
H, O

45-inch scarf tied asymmetrically
H, O

45-inch scarf worn as a throw
H, O, A, X

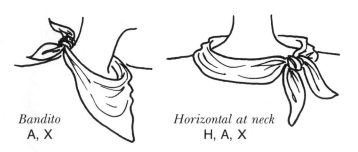

Bandito
A, X

Horizontal at neck
H, A, X

SCARF TREATMENTS

*Long narrow scarf
tied in a bow*
H, A, X

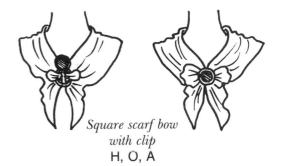

*Square scarf bow
with clip*
H, O, A

*Inside-out
knotted ascot*
A, H

*18-inch scarf or 36-inch scarf
rolled as a headband*
H, O, A, X

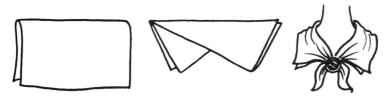

Making a collar from a square
A, X

*Knotted as a
turban wrap*
H, O, A, X

GLOVES

In days of old, gloves were buttoned with button hooks. The buttons began at the widest part of the thumb joint and were spaced at 1-inch intervals. Hence gloves came to be identified by button-lengths. Long white kid gloves worn for formal wear (usually by debutantes) are "eighteen-button gloves" while short wristlets are "one-button gloves." Here are some up-to-date glove tips:

• White kid gloves are only for after-five wear.
• Simple dark and medium-toned gloves are best for daytime.
• White cotton gloves are summer gloves (they are not worn for daytime in big cities like New York).
• Pigskin and thick suedes and leathers are for casual wear only.
• Doeskin is dressier and can be worn day or night. Cotton and nylon also can be worn day or night.
• Thin, elegant leather lined in silk is very warm.
• Bright-colored gloves make the hips seem bigger and are therefore better for **H** and **O** bodies than for **A** and **X** types.
• Inexpensive lace gloves can look tacky, although at times they are "in" for very trendy looks.
• Sleek black suede gloves are for evening.
• Startling wristlets or other wrist trims make the arms look shorter.
• Novelty wool gloves in colors should be coordinated with a scarf, hat or jewelry (Rule of Two).

In general, glove color should match:

• Your shoes or bag.
• Your costume. Be precise—there are many shades of red, blue, etc. A tint or shade (pale gray or charcoal with a gray suit) will also work.
• Your coat.
• The vivid contrast color of your scarf or hat (Rule of Two).
• Nothing in your costume—this works for neutral gloves (white, beige or black) only.

GLASSES AND SUNGLASSES

Eyeglass frames should be chosen to work with your wardrobe and hair coloring. For example, I like black (Winter) or white (Summer) frames and tortoise shell (I have brown hair).

- Frame size and shape should be in proportion to your face shape:
  - Oval shape—Any size
  - Square shape—Round or angled up, but never square
  - Diamond or heart shape—Less wide than the temple
  - Round—Square frames that sweep out and up at the brow
  - Long—Glasses can be wider than the face and fairly large to break up length.
  - High bridges make the nose seem longer and vice-versa.

- All glasses should be kept in cases so they don't get scratched. Scratched glasses are not only bad for your eyes, they look dirty and contribute to a sloppy look.
- Cheap sunglasses can be damaging to the eyes because the plastic may distort images and cause eye strain. Also, many sunglasses have dark lenses that do not screen out harmful ultraviolet rays. Good sunglasses are worth the cost, and can be worn with a rope if you are prone to losing them (as I am).

Frames of eyeglasses and sunglasses should be selected with face shape in mind. These flatter (from the top) oval, heart-shaped, square, round and oblong faces.

HANDBAGS

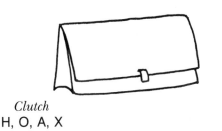

Clutch
H, O, A, X

Evening
H, O, A, X

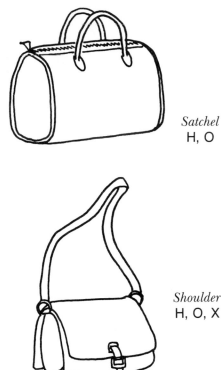

Satchel
H, O

Shoulder
H, O, X

Handled purse
H, O, A, X

Tote
H, O, X

HANDBAGS

- If you are building a wardrobe of good bags, choose a color which goes with most of your clothes (black, brown, beige, white).
- If you are a businesswoman and carry a briefcase, try a medium-sized bag and an attache or tote. This not only looks neater but saves your back, neck and shoulders. (Heavy bags can lead to curvature of the spine).
- A good basic bag wardrobe should have:
  - One evening bag.
  - One good daytime bag.
  - One tote or attache.
- When I buy a bag, I first check to be sure my contents will fit. I remove the paper and put all my handbag contents into it (get a salesclerk before someone calls security).

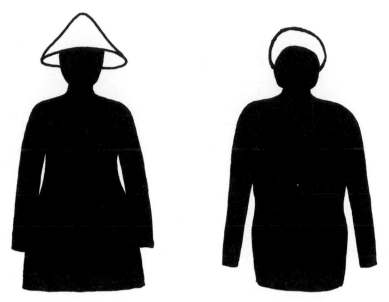

*Don't wear a hat that repeats a line that you are trying to de-emphasize in your body or face, as with this **A**-shape and **O**-shape.*

HATS

- A hat should never repeat an aspect of your shape you are trying to de-emphasize. For example, **A** types don't wear coolie hats and **O**'s don't wear bowl-shaped cloches.
- The brim of a large hat should never be wider than your shoulder line or it will ruin your balanced look.
- The best hat hairdo seems to be the chin-length bob or nape ponytail. Short hair, however, looks good with many hats—cossack and beret styles, for example. A hat's width should never be less than your hairdo's widest part (it will look like a peanut on a log).
- Make sure a hat fits comfortably. One Easter I wore a too-tight cloche and had a headache for days. As an **O** I should have known better anyway. I looked like an Easter egg!
- Choose a hat whose style is in keeping with the mood of your outfit. For example, flowered bonnets and hats with veils don't work with business suits.

Don't wear hats that are wider than your shoulders or narrower than your hair silhouette.

HOSIERY

"If they asked me, I could write a book . . ."

I am a hosiery nut. Hosiery is one area of accessories many women tend to neglect, which is a shame. In this section I'm going to explain some hosiery "facts of life": what to look for, what to expect from different constructions, and how to get the right fit. Then I'll explain how to use hosiery as a fashion accessory.

TYPES OF HOSIERY

Like most things, hosiery involves trade-offs. In a perfect world most of us would like hosiery that is so sheer it's virtually invisible (in beige shades), fits perfectly, feels wonderful, and wears forever without picking or running. Unfortunately, we live in an imperfect world. The sheerest hosiery yarns are also the most fragile and the poorest fitting. The yarns that fit, wear and feel the best are less sheer. Interlocking stitches that prevent runs also greatly reduce sheerness (and do not prevent holes or picks). Sheerness is not related to quality, it is related to the yarn used in the garment. Choose the hosiery that comes closest to meeting your needs for durability or sheerness based on the occasion in question.

The yarns used in hosiery fall into four main groups. These are as follows:

- *Ultra sheers* are made of fine nylon yarns that are very sheer but don't stretch much. Consequently they fit and wear more poorly than heavier yarns.
- *Day sheers* are made of slightly heavier nylon yarns that stretch moderately, and consequently fit and wear fairly well.
- *Spandex sheers* (also called Lycra sheers, silken sheers, etc.) are made of fine nylon yarn in combination with fine spandex yarns (spandex is very elastic and imparts a silky, clingy quality to the garment). These offer a wonderful combination of sheerness (but less than ultra sheers), with good fit and durability. Spandex yarns also impart a sheen to the leg, which I love.
- *Support hosiery* is made of nylon in combination with heavy spandex yarns to give hosiery a great deal of compression and support. Naturally this reduces the sheerness of the garment. As with spandex sheers, support hosiery gives a distinct sheen to the leg. The same heavy spandex fibers, when used only in the panty portion, give control-top pantyhose its compressing (and slimming) power. Support yarns are also the most durable of all hosiery types, and wonderful for women who are on their legs a lot.

Other construction features to look for in pantyhose are a cotton-crotch panel for comfort and shaped leg boarding. Boarded hosiery comes in flat packages and has the shape of the leg set into the garment. Although it does not affect the pantyhose significantly, boarding does impart a soft feel to the hosiery and is less likely to chafe.

HOSIERY SIZING

The *package* is your key to getting the right product. The most important thing you can do to get the right pantyhose is take time to read the package. Once you've read the front of the package and selected the right style (non-support, control top, support, textures) refer to the size chart that is on back of nearly all hosiery packages.

Using the size chart is fairly simple. Find your correct height and weight on the grid or table, and buy the size indicated for that combination. The size chart tells you a lot about how well the hosiery will fit. Generally speaking, the more sizes, the better. A brand that uses five sizes to cover a given height and weight range will fit you significantly better than a brand that uses only two sizes to cover the same fit range.

The bigger the size range claimed, the poorer the hosiery will fit if you fall into the height and weight categories around the edges of the grid for your size. If you are in the upper range for a given size (between two sizes), the larger of the sizes will fit you more comfortably (unless you are a particularly slim-legged and slim-hipped O). There is no advantage in trying to squeeze into a smaller size—it will only make you uncomfortable. Once you have the garment on, no one will know what size you are wearing. Wear the one you will be most comfortable in and that will give you the most confidence.

In addition to the size chart, hosiery packages contain fabric content (see above section on yarns) as well as washing instructions. Although washing hosiery by hand is recommended by many manufacturers, many women get excellent results by placing their hosiery in a mesh bag and throwing it into the washing machine with their clothes.

USING HOSIERY AS A FASHION ACCESSORY

Using hosiery creatively is a very low-cost, effective way to update an old outfit or make a daytime outfit do double duty in the evening. This is an area many of you neglect because it's scary. You wonder whether you will look stunning or ridiculous and sometimes that can be a fine line, but I'm going to give you some pointers that will help you achieve a wonderful look that you are comfortable with.

- Match your hose and shoes to the bottom of your hem (in value if not in exact color) to look taller. Contrast your hem, hose and shoes to look shorter. (Exception: White or cream hose with black patent is *always* a winner—who cares about height when you look that good?
- Never wear hosiery with runs ("No one will notice." Oh, yeah?) or with "tiny" little holes in the crotch. By day's end you will be walking like a cowboy with saddle sores (Gary Cooper, wincing). Need I say more?
- Get out of the habit of wearing hose the color of your skin; try colors and textures. Here are a few ways to do so:
  - *The finished leg:* Hose and shoes match and are the same color or value (lightness or darkness) as the hem.
  - *The contrast leg:* Hose color is in sharp contrast to the hem and shoes, which in turn, match in color or value. This works well with dark hose and spectator shoes.
  - *The contrast leg and shoes:* Hose and shoes are the same color and value and are sharply contrasted to the hem. Light hose and shoes will widen a leg, while dark will slim—I do both and love both looks.
  - *The high-fashion leg:* The hose are of a surprise color and/or texture; the color should be repeated elsewhere.

Here are some basic suggestions on how to wear and use specific colors to get that fashionable look:

- *Black* is a true neutral. It goes well with many things and does not call attention to a larger leg. Do not wear pale sandals or shoes with black hose (spectators are the exception here). Black hose and shoes add sophistication to bright or primary-color dresses (reds, yellows, blues, etc.),

HOSIERY TREATMENTS

The monotone leg:
Hose and shoe match hem.

The contrast leg:
Hose contrasts with hem and shoes.

The contrast leg and shoes:
Hose and shoes contrast with hem.

The high-fashion leg:
Hose color is repeated
in the scarf
(Accessory Rule of Two).

so don't be afraid to mix them up. Black also looks chic with dark green, wine, brown and blue.

- *White/off white* look perfect with pastels and with neutrals for a change from a "natural" leg. For a stylish look, combine these colors with black and red, turquoise, bright yellow, cobalt blue and other brights.
- *Non-beige neutrals* such as khaki, putty, taupe, green-gray and green-brown are chameleon colors that adapt to match somewhat related colors. They look well with browns, grays, taupes, etc., and contrast well with wine, dark green and black.
- *Grays* match almost anything, but here is a word of caution: Be careful when mixing gray with other grays, blues or pinks. Some grays are quite blue and others quite pink, and all look best when matched with their own color family.
- *Blues* cover a wide range of colors. Navy goes well with red, white, pinks, wines, light grays and classic plaids. Medium blues also look good with white (excluding shoes), red, wine, dark greens, grays and black. Pale blues are hard to

wear except when matched to a specific outfit or other pastels. Grays and pinks look better.

- *Reds* complement the other neutral colors (black and white). Bright reds give life and excitement to darks and ordinary neutrals.

- *Texture and pattern hosiery* can give you a very fashionable, sophisticated look with less mix-and-match trauma than colors. For example, sophisticated black textured hose can turn a daytime outfit into a glamorous evening outfit. Large-sized women have some special needs when it comes to textures however, and here are some rules of thumb in choosing textured and patterned pantyhose.

  o Non-directional patterns are safest. A pattern that randomly repeats itself on the leg, such as dots, checks or geometrics, will look sophisticated anywhere on the leg.

  o Vertical ribbing may or may not look good on your particular legs depending on the proportion of the ankle and the calf. "Stripes" that start out narrow and sophisticated at your ankle may end up very wide if you have heavy calves. This draws attention to an area you may not want to accentuate.

  o Horizontal patterns should be avoided unless you have the height and slim legs to carry them off. They tend to make your legs look wider and shorter.

  o Lace hosiery is an option, but consider the proportion of your legs before you invest money in this fashion accent. Here again, the pattern may look radically different in the calf area than it does in the ankle area.

Finally, don't be afraid to experiment with hosiery. Try different brands to discover one that works best for you. The non-beige neutrals are perfectly acceptable in any social situation and for many business occasions. Textures and patterns add pizazz to any outfit for a special look. And if you're unsure about a combination,

SHOE WARDROBE BASICS

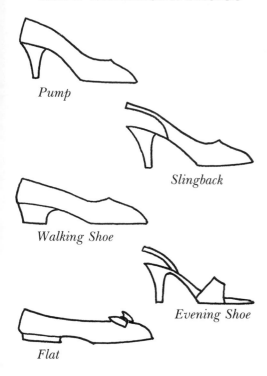

Pump

Slingback

Walking Shoe

Evening Shoe

Flat

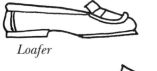

Loafer

Espadrille

Sneaker

Boot

don't wear it because your lack of confidence will be perceived by others and prevent you from carrying off the look.

SHOES

There are three words to sum up shoes: "FIT, FIT and FIT!" If your feet hurt, you are miserable—and there is no way you can look your best when you are miserable. If you are torn between two sizes, go to the larger size—vanity in shoe buying can be harmful to your feet. Further, if you need shoes wider than a B (medium) width, go to any extreme to track them down.

Walking shoes (1½-inch heel, preferably stacked and made of indestructible wood) are an orthopedic and comfort necessity in cities where walking is a pleasurable necessity. Women who have H, O or X body types with a high center of gravity must be especially careful not to wear shoes that make them teeter as they are more likely to fall.

Well-cared-for shoes are essential to your total look. Runover shoes are not only unsightly, but dangerous, as they can cause you to fall. If you don't have a good cobbler, find one who can:

- Alter a shoe that is too big or a bit narrow.
- Fix heels, soles and sock linings on beloved shoes.
- Restore shine and luster to worn shoes.
- Save you a fortune.

Good shoes are expensive, so I recommend keeping it simple and building a summer and winter shoe wardrobe of the following shoes:

PUMPS OR SLINGBACK*
1 black leather
1 white/bone
1 black suede
1 black patent
1 pair spectators (optional)

*Keep them open at the instep (ankle and T-straps shorten)

WALKING SHOE
1 neutral color

EVENING SHOE
1 universal color (black, gold or silver)

FUN SHOES*
1 pair summer
1 pair winter

*Flats, wedges, espadrilles, loafers or low-instep oxfords

BOOTS
1 pair all weather

ATHLETIC
1 pair durable sneakers

SHOULDER PADS

Although shoulder pads are technically daywear lingerie, they can alter a garment's form and have as much to do with changing its look as any accessory. For that reason, we discuss them in this chapter. However, because they are basic to any wardrobe, they are discussed further in Chapter 14, *Organizing and Planning Your Wardrobe.* Shoulder pads:

- Make wide hips seem narrower.
- Make full breasts seem less so.
- Make a thick waist smaller.

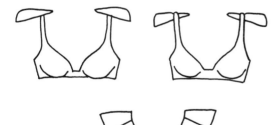

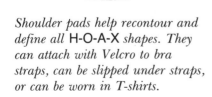

Shoulder pads help recontour and define all H-O-A-X *shapes. They can attach with Velcro to bra straps, can be slipped under straps, or can be worn in T-shirts.*

Shoulder pads with Velcro attached to slip over the bra can be purchased in lingerie departments. Larger or smaller pads can be made by buying uncovered pads in the sewing store and sliding them under your bra strap. Most stores now carry lacy T-shirts with shoulder pads, and these are easy and comfortable to wear. I occasionally attach larger pads with Velcro onto these T-shirts for a more pronounced shoulder. This is easier than pinning pads into every outfit.

11

Balancing Your Line with Great-Looking Hair

Is hair important to balancing your figure? You bet! As with hats, your hairstyle should not repeat the body shape that you are trying to de-emphasize. Mary's O shape is accentuated by the hairstyle at top; the second hairstyle is far more flattering.

HAIR HAS BECOME the ultimate accessory for today's fashions. Your appearance is not complete unless your hair conveys the same mood and fashion sense as your clothing. Hair presents us with a wonderful tool for rebalancing the figure and for making a definitive style statement.

Recently, I met a very petite woman who was a student of medieval atudies. Her hair was Rapunzel-long and plaited down her back—absolutely perfect for the major interest in her life and flattering to her round pretty face and delicate curvy figure. So maybe I should grow my hair long enough to hang out the window of my eleventh-floor apartment? No way!

My hair drives me nuts! Well, actually, it's not my hair—it's me. Whenever I'm bored and looking for a psychological lift, I start to fixate on what I could do with my hair. The usual answer is to grow it out to the chin-length bob I had for most of my life—1956 to 1982, to be precise. It takes no shrink to analyze that this pipe dream is a reversion to the past, but once every year or so, I try to grow my hair longer. Halfway through the process, I look like a kewpie doll and run to the hairdresser to cut it short. The next day I tell all the people who have listened to me obsess over my locks that I really like short hair best. I'm fine for 6 months or so, until my next "growathon" madness begins.

Well, not any more. Something has changed in my approach to my hair. I have a new friend, Brigitte Grosjean, who is an executive for Glemby Salons. One day I was moaning about my hair, and Brigitte said,

Lilliana, an **A**, *thought her short hair didn't look neat, so sides were cut and the top was given a partial perm to help hold the face-slimming height. Her hair was blown dry with mousse in an upsweep to give height to her round face.*

GROUP 1

A: You need simple, shiny, no-fuss, short or medium hair with an excellent cut (blunt or layered) to reflect the shine. For additional shine, you may want to try a gloss, henna or cellophane and you may wish to voluminize or modernize your hair with a root perm. Long, straight hair tends to age women over 25.

B: Full, glamorous and feminine is most important to you, so your hair should be medium or long, wavy or curly. These looks require time, but a perm or partial perm may help to cut care time. Wavy or curly hair does not reflect shine as much as straight hair does, so medium- or lighter-colored hair may benefit from some color highlighting or a brightening process.

C: Versatility is important to you, as you want to have the option to change your look at a moment's notice. Medium or long lengths suit you best. Volume, shine and styling time problems can be solved with root or semiperms, glosses or highlighting.

GROUP 2

D: You would look best in a short haircut which can be worn straight and simple or blown dry with mousse or gel for an upsweep. Root perms for volume and gloss or highlighting for color and brightness may be useful.

E: Short or medium styles are best for you. If your hair is thin or straight, you may find bangs, body waves, highlighting, mousses and gels helpful. Hot rollers or a curling iron will give you a wavy look, but you will need additional support from some combination of perm, mousse, gel and "spritz" (spray that really holds). Blow-drying can also work for you and afford you versatility of style.

F: Medium to long hair is what you want, with lots of fullness and soft wave or curl. Because such hairdos require extra time to maintain, you should have naturally curly hair or a good perm or partial perm. Many of the new perms are meant to be "wash and go," giving you a modern, natural, tousled look.

X *Tara wanted to lose her college-girl look. A short layered cut and a root perm for volume updated her look. Gel was used to finish and hold the brushed-forward look.*

Gabrielle, an **A**, *had extraordinarily strong features that needed a bit of softening. Shorter bangs and softer layers were cut, and her hair was blown dry with mousse.*

GROUP 3

G: You should definitely consider one of the many exciting color options available today.

H: You should talk to your hairdresser about a perm.

YOUR HAIRCUT SHOULD FLATTER YOUR FACE

Having the right haircut—one that's fashionable yet feminine—is the biggest confidence booster for any woman. Great-looking hair makes you look and feel good and can help balance your figure.

What is the right style for you? A great haircut is basic to any hairstyle. Whether you have curly, straight, wavy or coarse hair, there's a style that's great for you, your personality and lifestyle. It may be one length or layered. Often, the cut is the style itself.

Just as the right makeup colors can flatter your face, so can the right haircut. To determine what is best for you, begin by pulling your hair off your face and examining its shape.

Is it:

	Yes or No
Round?	_____
Square?	_____
Oval?	_____
Diamond/Heart?	_____
Oblong?	_____
Triangular?	_____

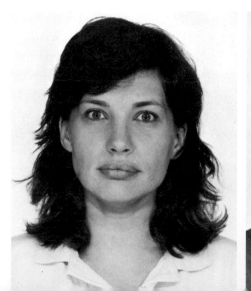

Do you have a:

High forehead?	_____
Low forehead?	_____
Low hairline on nape of neck?	_____
Short neck?	_____
Dowager's hump?	_____
Small chin?	_____
Large nose?	_____
Protuberant ears?	_____
Long neck?	_____
Protuberant jaw?	_____
Fleshy full face?	_____
Full or slackening jowls?	_____
Double chin?	_____
Deep line between nose and mouth?	_____

O *faces are almost always very full. Audrey's hair was given a soft perm for volume, blown dry with mousse and brushed off the face.*

I believe that all face shapes, as body shapes, have a beauty of their own. Nevertheless, many women want to make their faces appear more oval. Here are some ways to do that:

ROUND FACE SHAPE

Description: Round in the cheeks and chin, it looks like a circle.
Goal: To elongate and narrow.
How:

- Side part
- Asymmetrical style
- Soft, wispy asymmetrical bangs
- Bob that cuts into the cheek
- Soft wisps on the temple, forehead and upper cheek
- Upswept lines
- Height on top
- Little volume at the sides
- Some fullness at the earline but hugging the back of the neck

SQUARE FACE SHAPE

Description: Forehead, cheeks and jaw are the same width (or close to it) and the face looks like a square or short rectangle. The jaw is square.

Goal: To round the angular or sharp appearance; to soften.

How:

- Side parts/diagonal parts
- Asymmetrical bangs
- Asymmetrical cuts
- Width at the forehead
- Width at jawline if the hair juts in at an angle or in soft curls and "cuts" the jawline
- Softly upswept lines
- Roundness or fullness in the crown
- Height

H *Deborah got a little carried away with growing out her hair. High bangs and a blunt page uplift and soften her square face, showing her beautiful bone structure. Very long hair is for the under-30 group.*

OVAL FACE SHAPE

Description: Egglike shape considered by beauty experts to be perfection. High cheekbones and narrow (but curved) chin are common.

Goal: To emphasize a blessing.

How: Can wear any hairdo soft or dramatic, simple or slick, full or fluffy.

HEART/DIAMOND FACE SHAPE

Description: Cheeks are full and abruptly narrow to a point. Diamond has a narrow forehead; heart has a wide forehead.

Goal: To increase the width of the jaw and distract from any forehead imbalance.

How:

- Bangs, especially fluffy bangs
- Asymmetrical fullness
- Fullness at the cheek and chin level
- Covered ears
- Blunt cut
- Soft wisps on the temple and cheek
- Fullness at the nape of the neck

OBLONG FACE SHAPE

Description: Longer than wide, often with hollow cheekbones and fullness at the jaw hinge.
Goal: To shorten and widen.
How:

- Bangs
- Volume and softness at the sides
- Medium length or somewhat long
- Softness to counteract angularity
- Simple midneck cuts

TRIANGULAR FACE SHAPE

Description: Wide jaw and chin in dramatic contrast to a narrow forehead.
Goal: To widen the forehead and narrow the chin and jaw.
How:

- Softly pulled back and up from the temple and forehead
- Chin-length cut
- Side part (low is good)
- Expose part of the forehead
- Asymmetrical bangs
- Bangs that go to temple wings
- Fullness at the temple and forehead
- Cuts that jut in to the jawline
- Curls or wisps that fall on the jawline

OTHER FACIAL FEATURES

In addition to the shape of your face, you may have other facial features that you want to de-emphasize with your hairstyle:

Feature: High forehead.
Solution: Long, soft bangs.

Feature: Low forehead.
Solution: Short, wispy bangs.

Feature: Low neck hairline.

Solution: Medium length hair or short hair cut in wisps to cover the hairline. DO NOT TRY WAXING. It is agony on the back of the neck. Electrolysis is preferable.

Feature: Short neck.

Solution: Hair cut close to the head on back and sides, or uplifted to create the illusion of air over the ears. Wisps combed forward on the neck will slim a thick neck.

Feature: Dowager's hump.

Solution: Medium-length haircut to cover the nape of the neck, or short hair that is not cut blunt at the back but is feathered and wispy.

Feature: Small, receding chin.

Solution: Fullness at the back of the crown and at the base of the neck.

Feature: Large nose.

Solution: Hair pulled back from the forehead, with rounded wispy bangs and fullness at the back of the neck; ponytail.

Feature: Protuberant ears.

Solution: Hair that covers all or most of the ears and medium or large earrings for balance.

Lucinda, an **A***, had hair that was too long and flat on top, so her bangs and crown were cut and blown dry with mousse.*

Amy, an **A**, *had curly hair that was long overdue for a cut. She wanted a long hairdo that would withstand New York's humid weather. Long layers were cut and dried naturally with gel, showing a lovely heart-shaped face.*

Feature: Long neck.
Solution: Fullness at the back of the neck, medium-length styles, chignons and neck-tied ponytail.

Feature: Protuberant jaw.
Solution: Hair cutting into the jawline.

Feature: Fleshy, full face.
Solution: Some hair combed along the sides of the face.

Feature: Full or slack jowls.
Solution: Lines that lift up over the ear, drawing the eye up.

Feature: Double chin.
Solution: Upswept styles and fullness at the top of the head and crown.

Feature: Nose-to-mouth line.
Solution: Hair cut or pulled away from the face so as not to reflect or repeat this line (as a soft chin-length pageboy might do, for instance).

CHOOSING AND MAINTAINING A HAIRSTYLE

With the active life of today's woman, a fashionable, easy-to-maintain hairstyle is a must. Words like "feminine" and "easy" define the hair looks of today. Fortunately, modern technology can help us achieve miracles. Now that you have assessed your preferences and analyzed your facial features, you are ready to choose the best style for you.

If you do not already have a superb hairdresser, you need to find one. Ask a friend whose hair you admire for a recommendation, or call Glemby at 1-800-821-7700 for the nearest of their 1,450 salons. They will do a free consultation.

Bring your hair chart (which you will complete at the end of this chapter). Tell the hairstylist that you want to talk before you snip, because you are looking for a long-term relationship (with a hairstylist—romance is another story). Discuss your chart and look for interest and enthusiasm in your stylist—otherwise, keep looking. If your chosen style requires that you grow out layers, your hairdresser can help you. You will need frequent trims, lest you look shaggy (I know all about that!) and you will need to learn to use mousses and gels to keep growing layers in place.

BASIC HAIRSTYLES: SHORT, MEDIUM, LONG

I believe that there are basically three hairstyles: short, medium and long. Styles that claim to be something else are usually too contrived and trendy to be flattering. My number one pet-peeve is hair that is short in the front and medium or long in the back—this is not a hairstyle but a lack of decision.

In addition to the three lengths, hair has body, form and line. Hair can be blunt or layered, full or flat, curly or straight. The overall shape of hair affects the visual image of the total body. It becomes the form of the head. The line within this form is the style line, which affects the face shape and features. Body simply refers to the texture of hair, which in turn affects what forms and style lines it will hold (although body can be affected by chemical treatments such as perms or coloring).

Hair is an overall accessory to the style of the woman. Since women usually opt for several different styles to go with their varied life roles, most are happy with hairstyles that have some easy versatility.

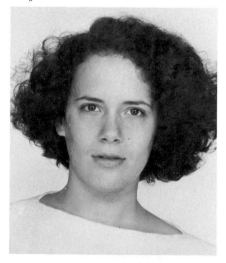

Three new looks for H *Greta's curly thick hair: (1) trimmed and dried with a diffuser; (2) with gel for a wet look; (3) up with a turban wrap and "Betty Grable" bang. All soften her look and show the beautiful angles of her face.*

SHORT HAIR

Blunt, short

Wedge

Boy cut

Teased, spritzed

Afro

Short hair needs a superb cut and should be trimmed every 4 weeks.

MEDIUM HAIR

Pageboy, blunt

Pageboy, layered

Bob, blunt

Bowl cut, tapered

Bowl cut, elongated, tapered

French bob, layered, permed

Pageboy, curly, blunt, set or permed

Pageboy, blunt, off face

Afro, medium layered, natural curl or permed

Flip, blunt, set

Medium hair may need perming and should be trimmed every 6 weeks.

LONG HAIR

1971 droop

Blunt, long

Layered, long

Layered, long, curly

Beauty-pageant "bouff"

French braid

Ponytail, high

Ponytail, low

Topknot

French twist

Chignon

Long Hair is rarely flattering if it is flat and lank (circa 1971 "golden oldie"). It benefits from perms and color, and needs trimming every 8 weeks.

PERMS AND COLOR

Do you want incredible body and volume? Try a perm or new color! With so many techniques available today, you can find one that will add more volume to your hair for a more updated, modern appearance.

Today, unlike in the past, perms are used as an accent to a haircut. No longer does a perm have to go all over the head. It can be given just where you need it. Even short haircuts look great with a body perm or a soft looser perm. The most exciting developments in perms are products that are packed with conditioners and gentle enough to use on color-highlighted hair! Perms no longer mean dull frizz!

If hair is very straight or fine, a soft body wave or perm just on top can give needed support and easy, natural-looking volume.

A root perm is another popular technique where only the roots are exposed to the perming solution. The result is hair that has more lift instead of lying flat to the scalp. Hair looks thicker and fuller but still smooth.

With all the new technology, hair-color treatments are now designed to enhance a hairstyle, not to cover it up. Color has become the great stylemaker . . . the ultimate accent to a great haircut. It can be applied so it softly highlights the hair around the face, or merely applied to the tips for natural-looking flashes of color. These free-handed strokes of color (or hair painting) can do wonders for any haircut or hair type. In addition, color can give limp or fine hair a look of fullness and body.

A skillful use of hair color can draw attention away from facial flaws while emphasizing good features. For example, introducing a darker tone to the sides of the face and adding a brighter, lighter shade to the hair above the forehead narrows a wide face.

Another trend includes glossing. This is an all-over, semipermanent color wash that brightens up dull-looking hair, leaving it shiny and vibrant without changing the natural hair color.

Gray and white hair can remain natural while being "cleaned and brightened" with new procedures.

Black hair can be cut to enhance its lovely natural curl or relaxed for straighter looks.

H *Liz thought she looked tired, so a "hair-cleaning" was done to brighten her gray hair. Her hair was then blown dry with a little gel, uplifting her face and emphasizing her cheekbones.*

MOUSSES AND GELS

The newest hair shapes are being created with products that give hair a new texture and finish for greater styling versatility. These new products are fun to use and easy to master—hair can be slicked, scrunched, spiked or fluffed into glamorous, dramatic looks.

Mousse is the most exciting of these products. Packaged in aerosol cans, this frothy, shaving-cream-like substance is perfect for adding body and fullness to even the finest hair—long or short.

For a tousled look, work mousse through wet hair and comb with fingers until dry. Or "scrunch" (squeezing fistfuls of hair into balls) hair while you blow dry. For a smooth shape, apply mousse and blow dry. Then add more mousse where you want a stronger line—hair behind ears, a side part swept up, etc. Brush in that direction.

Gel delivers a firmer hold than mousse. It's thicker, stickier and has real holding power. It can be used on wet or dry hair and lets you mold, sculpt and slick a hairstyle. Lots of gel results in the "wet" look; less gel gives a softer but slicker-than-mousse look.

For spiky bangs, apply gel to wet hair and blow dry. Then reapply, pulling hair out in various directions with fingers. For the wet look, coat hair with gel, finger-comb and allow to dry.

Hair sprays have been around for years. But with the need for sleeker hairstyles, sprays such as setting lotions and thermal stylers are in demand. Unlike hair sprays of old, these new products give softer hold and are great humidity fighters.

SETS, SPECIAL EFFECTS AND HAIRPIECES

The wet set of yesteryear is rarely used today. If you have a weekly wash, tease, bouff and spray job—and then sleep in hairnets and toilet paper until the next

H *Teri had long curly hair that had a 1970s look to it. Her hair was cut into a blunt, elongated bowl with a low bang to emphasize her eyes. Her hair was dried with mousse.*

Hair doo-dads and hairpieces. Use hairpieces to balance the figure by adding volume. They attract the eye—and distract from your shape—by making your hair look wonderful.

go-round with the hairdryer—you need to update your look. In fact, you need it fast!

Electric curlers, curling irons, blow-dryers and diffusers are easy to use and are the modern tools for special effects.

Hairpieces and hair ornaments are wonderful for quick polished looks or for special occasions. Bows, headbands and combs work well on all lengths of hair and on all ages. Care must be taken, however, to coordinate hairpieces and ornaments with the overall style of an outfit.

X *Lill wanted an update, so her hair was cut into subtle layers and blown dry with mousse for a natural look.*

HAIR INVENTORY

This inventory will help you pull together all the facts you need to choose the right hairstyle. Fill it out and discuss it with your hairstylist.

My face shape: _____

My current style: _____

The style I want to have: _____

Alternate styles with this basic style: _____

_____

_____

My hair color: _____

My color needs: _____

_____

Color ideas to try: _____

_____

My hair volume (thin, medium or thick): _____

My hair texture (fine, medium or coarse): _____

My hair curve (straight, wavy or curly): _____

Perm ideas to try: _____

_____

My scalp type (dry, average or oily): _____

How often do I wash my hair? _____

What conditioners do I use? _____

_____

What gels, mousses and sprays do I like? _____

_____

What hairpieces and wigs do I like? _____

_____

What hair ornaments do I like? _____

_____

_____

Casual styles I can do: _____

_____

Career styles I can do: _____

_____

Dressy styles I can do: _____

12

Finishing Your Look with Makeup

I LOVE WARPAINT. Many women hate it, and some are afraid of it because some others overdo it. Unlike hair, makeup can do little to balance the overall impression of your shape. I include this chapter, however, because makeup can and should do two very important things for you: (1) distract from the less wonderful parts of you by bringing the eye to the face, where the personality is best reflected, and (2) make you look much more attractive.

My agency has a "resident" makeup and beauty expert named Deborah Steele. She has a wealth of knowledge to share. Press a button and out comes a lifetime of no-nonsense tips. Deborah believes in basic healthy skin care and simple makeup. She agrees with me that many women wear too little or no makeup for fear that they might wear too much and look foolish, so she has put together a simple program: four steps for skin care and five steps for perfect makeup.

We begin (you're used to this by now, aren't you?) with a questionnaire to bring into focus your own needs and preferences. Place a check by everything that applies to you.

Hair and makeup artist Deborah Steele adds last-minute touches at a photo shoot. Deborah believes in simple makeup techniques to emphasize the best facial features and draw attention away from facial and figure problems.

SKIN AND MAKEUP QUESTIONNAIRE

SKIN TYPE

☐ Normal   ☐ Acne
☐ Oily   ☐ Allergies
☐ Dry   ☐ Other
☐ Combination

SKIN ANALYSIS

	Forehead	Eyes	Nose	Mouth	Chin	Neck	Cheeks
Wrinkles	☐	☐	☐	☐	☐	☐	☐
Blackheads	☐	☐	☐	☐	☐	☐	☐
Large pores	☐	☐	☐	☐	☐	☐	☐
Whiteheads	☐	☐	☐	☐	☐	☐	☐
Dryness	☐	☐	☐	☐	☐	☐	☐
Oiliness	☐	☐	☐	☐	☐	☐	☐
Redness	☐	☐	☐	☐	☐	☐	☐
Pimples	☐	☐	☐	☐	☐	☐	☐
Flabbiness	☐	☐	☐	☐	☐	☐	☐
Freckles	☐	☐	☐	☐	☐	☐	☐
Age spots	☐	☐	☐	☐	☐	☐	☐

SKIN COLOR

☐ Ivory   ☐ Olive
☐ Beige   ☐ Dark Beige
☐ Ruddy   ☐ Brown
☐ Yellow   ☐ Dark Brown

EYES

☐ Blue   ☐ Average
☐ Green   ☐ Close together
☐ Gray   ☐ Wide-set
☐ Hazel   ☐ Droopy lids
☐ Brown   ☐ Bags
☐ Black   ☐ Turned down corners
☐ Large
☐ Small

BROWS & LASHES

Space between lash and brow:

☐ Short   ☐ Medium brows
☐ Average   ☐ Long lashes
☐ Thick brows   ☐ Medium lashes
☐ Thin brows   ☐ Short lashes

MOUTH

☐ Average   ☐ Full lower lip
☐ Pretty   ☐ Wide
☐ Thin   ☐ Cupid's bow
☐ Full   ☐ Small (rosebud)

NOSE

☐ Large   ☐ Turned up
☐ Small   ☐ Turned down
☐ Medium   ☐ Broad
☐ Curved   ☐ Narrow
☐ Crooked   ☐ Crease to mouth

CHEEKS

☐ Full   ☐ Average
☐ Contoured   ☐ Flabby

TEETH

☐ Straight   ☐ White
☐ Crooked   ☐ Yellow
☐ Ivory

The most universally flattering makeup accomplishes the following: (1) evens the skin tones; (2) emphasizes the eyes; (3) adds subtle glowy blush to the cheeks; and (4) shapes a pretty mouth.

COURTESY JEFF FLAX

CHIN

☐ Small ☐ Double
☐ Prominent ☐ Dimpled
☐ Fleshy

JAW

☐ Firm ☐ Jowly
☐ Flabby

BEST FEATURES

_____

_____

WORST FEATURES

_____

_____

SKIN CARE

Now that you have a clearer picture of your best and worst facial and skin features, you need to determine the proper skin-care routines and dedicate yourself to them religiously. Beautiful skin is the basis of a beautiful face.

Hair can do more to balance the overall impression of the body than makeup, which influences style more than form. Lill (left) is a soft feminine type, and Greta is a more angular, high-fashion type. Each model's makeup helps her achieve her look.

Basic skin care consists of:

- Cleansing (morning and evening)
- Freshening (morning and evening)
- Moisture (morning and evening)
- Facial (weekly)

The following chart shows you which products are best for different skin types.

SKIN CARE PRODUCTS

CLEANSER	*Dry*	*Oily*	*Normal[1]*
Soap and water		√	√
Cleansing lotion	√	√	√
Cleansing cream	√		
Water-soluble foaming cleanser	√	√	√
Facial scrub		√	√
FRESHENER			
Mild	√		√[2]
Strong (with alcohol)		√	√[3]
MOISTURE			
Night cream	√	√[4]	√
Light moisture (daytime)	√[5]	√	√

[1]Combination skin does the oily skin procedures in T-zone only.
[2]Winter only   [4]Light application
[3]Summer only   [5]Heavy application

WEEKLY FACIALS

We have seen all sorts of home remedies, from facials that require you to be a chemist to the truly outrageous cod-liver oil (bad if you have cats) or molasses (not great in fly season). Deborah even found one that sounded like a perfect recipe for guacamole. Make a double batch and serve with corn chips! Here is the facial I have been doing for years:

EASY AT-HOME FACIAL

1. Steam skin. (Do not burn. I use a warm wash cloth or steaming water.)

2. Use shortening or vegetable oil to loosen surface dirt.
3. Gently massage skin with a grainy scrub or a paste of salt and a little warm water to unclog pores (salt is great for deep-cleansing oily skin).
4. Splash face with warm water.
5. Massage face gently with night cream (or shortening, believe it or not).
6. Remove excess cream. Apply witch hazel or your favorite freshener with a cotton ball.
7. Apply your favorite mask or make a mask of:
   - Egg white for oily skin.
   - Egg yolk for dry skin.
   - Whole egg for normal or combination skin.
8. Let dry and remove with cool water.

This hot and cold facial is a favorite of one of my models:

HOT AND COLD FACIAL

1. Moisturize a clean face.
2. Steam for 1 minute.
3. Apply a mask (beaten egg).
4. Remove mask.
5. Rub alcohol or witch hazel on your face.
6. Run an ice cube over your face.
7. Moisturize again.

If you have skin problems such as acne, whiteheads, moles, or pores that are clogged or enlarged, see a dermatologist and work on improving your skin. Skin is the basis of all facial beauty and well worth the time and effort. Dermatologists can work miracles. More information on skin care is included in Chapter 13, *Professional Grooming and Model Tips.*

MAKEUP: THE 5 STEPS

1. Wash hands. Cleanse, freshen and moisturize your face and neck.
2. Use a foundation base that matches your skin color. Apply it with a cosmetic sponge. *Blend.* Use concealer underneath your eye area (don't rub) and on blemishes (a cotton swab is a great applicator). Use a

Tools of the Trade

big powder brush to apply loose translucent powder and, in hot weather, set makeup by briefly applying a damp face cloth or spritzing with a water atomizer.

3. Use blush that is similar in color (but lighter) to your chosen lip color. Brush it just below your cheekbone out to your temple and then back over the top of your cheek. *Blend.* This is the only place to use blush. (See the opposite page for notes on contouring with blush.)

4. Use a soft color eye shadow on your entire lid and eyebone region. *Blend.* Fill in your brows with brow color and brush them. Apply eyeliner to your upper lid at the lash line, and put mascara on both upper and lower lids.

5. Line your mouth with a lipliner to keep lip color from running, and apply lipstick.

You're gorgeous—and in 10 minutes!

MAKEUP PRODUCTS AND TECHNIQUES

BASE CONCEALER AND POWDER

Base should match your skin tone, and concealer should be one shade lighter. If concealer is too light, you'll look like a skunk (not to be confused with a raccoon, which is how I look when my eye makeup smears). Base comes in many forms:

- *Heavy coverage* gives a flawless finish.
- *Water base* is for oily skin.
- *Oil-absorbing* is for oily skin or for normal skin during summer.
- *Light/medium coverage* gives a sheer to average finish.
- *Powder/base* includes both finishes in one makeup.
- *Powder*, which should be translucent and not have frosty flecks (save that for New Year's Eve).

BLUSH AND CONTOURING

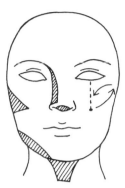

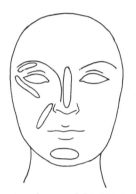

Contouring and highlighting should be used sparingly and blended well.

Blush goes on the cheek for color glow and warmth and does not belong (on anyone but models and actresses under bright lights) under your chin, across your nose or on your forehead.

Makeup should make you look prettier. Contouring is primarily for experts, because nine times out of ten it backfires, looking more like mud-gashes or day-old eggplant than like contouring.

If you must contour, use the lightest contour powder (buffers) you can find and mix it with translucent powder on your brush. This same "lightening" trick will work to soften a blush color. Blend very carefully and be sure you have a good mirror and light source. Powder and color blush go over contour.

Following are contour techniques used to minimize specific facial areas:

- Wide jaw: Apply blush along the jawbone and blend.
- Double chin: Contour in a "V" from the fleshy part of the curve under the fleshy part of the cheek, ending under the middle of the eye. Highlight on the very top of the cheekbone.
- Wide nose: Brush blush down the sides of the nose and highlight the center.
- Long nose: Put blush under the tip of the nose and highlight above the tip.
- Small chin: Use highlighter on the chin.
- Hooked nose: Contour at the bridge and on the tip.
- Nose to mouth crease: Paint highlighter with a thin brush, pat with your finger and powder.

No contour will make a fat face seem thin. Your goal is to look pretty—not dirty! No gashes or racing stripes!

LIP COLOR

Match lip liner to lip color. It should never be darker unless you are trying to make your mouth seem larger. I do not like lip corrections any more than I like

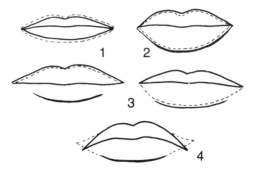

Lip contouring: (1) For a thin mouth, go over the lip line with lip color; (2) For too-full lips, use makeup base on the outer edges of the lips and don't take color quite to the edges; (3) If one lip is too full or too thin, use the same techniques (1 or 2); (4) For a mouth with turned-down corners, paint the corners slightly up.

contouring, but if you must make your mouth look bigger, smaller, etc., do it very subtly. The best lip makeup is lipstick that is on your lips and not in your purse. Color and shine light up a woman's face.

The illustrations show how to change the shape of your mouth with lipliner and lipstick. You should proceed carefully, however, lest you look like Joan Crawford in 1945.

EYES

Again, fancy eyeshadow applications are for the experts. To this day, I cannot do my makeup the way that Deborah does it. Nevertheless, I manage to get through life looking quite respectable.

Brows should have an arch and some volume—the penciled brow died with Jean Harlow. Brows should have an arch but not cause the face to look perpetually surprised like Lucille Ball. Shadows can be applied in one, two or three shades, but leave the twelve-tone polka-dot numbers and July 4th commemoratives for those crazy people who dream up cosmetic ads. If you do not have much space between your lashes and brow, keep the shadow treatment very simple.

Brows should begin about 1/4-inch closer to your nose than the inner corner of your eye and end on an imaginary straight line drawn from the bridge of your nose past the outer corner of your eye.

You may apply shadow with sponge-tip applicators or a narrow brush (1/3-inch to 5/8-inch wide). I prefer the wider brush because it is faster, lighter and more even.

For a one-tone, medium-light eyeshadow treatment, apply a lid color in any eyeshadow color. If you wish to highlight under the brow, use white, off-white, oyster, beige, or any other light, almost-white color. Highlighter is used to accent the shape of your eyebrows, so don't use it unless your eyebrows are well-shaped. Eye liner should be applied in a thin line at the lash line and not extend far beyond the outer corner of the eye.

For more elaborate shadow treatments, contour lines should be well-blended and in non-iridescent tones. *The secret of beautiful eyeshadow is proper blending!* Never leave

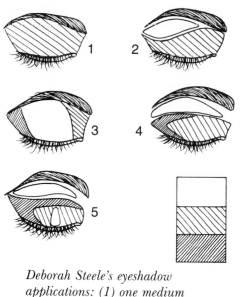

Deborah Steele's eyeshadow applications: (1) one medium color; (2) one medium, one light color; (3, 4, 5) one medium, one light, one deep (non-frosted) shadow.

stripes of color on the eyes—always blend. All blending is done outward toward the temple. Use fingertips, cotton swabs, sponges or applicators to blend.

At left are some winning eyeshadow treatments.

MAKEUP COLORS

Deborah says all women can wear either light/delicate colors, medium colors or dark dramatic colors. The variables are (1) your coloring, (2) your outfit and (3) the mood you are trying to create.

Manufacturers, methinks, stay up nights thinking up names for their makeup shades. From Revlon's "Little Red Russet," which is a great name for a great color, to some of the European imports that change names for American consumption to some form of French yet unknown to the *Academie Francaise*, I think this industry has a vivid imagination.

On the inside covers of this book, I have given you a chart of generic makeup hues. Deborah has made up a more detailed list below using generic color names. She divides her colors for light, medium and dark colorings, but says that she will often go a shade darker for contour or a tint lighter for highlight for any given skin tone. Further, she recommends that you keep colors softer for daytime and brighter or more intense for evening special effects.

LIPS*

Hue	Light Coloring	Medium Coloring	Dark Coloring
Brown	Soft rosy tan	Medium rosy tan	Frosted dark pink-brown
	Medium beige-peach	Medium brown & lavender	Cinnamon
Pink	Candy pink	Hot pink	Dark rose
	Frosty lavender	Frosty blue-pink	Dark pink-red
Corals/orange	Light bright coral	Medium coral	Deep red orange
	Clear pink coral	Medium coral & rose	Russet
Red	Light bright red	Clear blue-red	Cranberry
	Soft rosy red	Clear bright red	Dull wine red

*Lip color and liner—clear gloss for all

COURTESY JEFF FLAX

COURTESY JEFF FLAX

COURTESY RODGERS

Soft, pretty daytime looks.

EYE COLORS

Eyeshadows should bring out (not match) eye color and work with skin and hair color. The following *flat shadows* are for lid, contour and highlight.

	Light Coloring	Medium Coloring	Dark Coloring
WARM TONES	Peach	Antique peach	Dark taupe
	Rose peach	Toast	Dark brown
COOL TONES	Beige	Gold	Russet
	Pale lavender	Rose	Deep magenta
	Khaki gray	Deep turquoise	Dark green
	Military blue	Dull purple	Dark gray-brown
			Wine

The following *frosted shadows* are for lid or highlight, but should never be used in the crease.

Hue	Light Coloring	Medium Coloring	Dark Coloring
Gold	Pale gold	Bright gold	Orange
Rose gold	Old rose	Coral rose	Deep rose-gold
Gray	Pearl gray	Banker's gray	Charcoal gray
Blue	Teal	Royal	Bright navy
Green	Olive	Breen	Moss
Camel	Light camel	Medium camel	Bronze
Caramel	Peach caramel	Caramel	Russet
Dusty rose	Pale mauve	Tea rose	Plum
Lavender	Lavender	Amethyst	Aubergine
Evening shimmer	Sheer gold	Silver	Gold

COURTESY JEFF FLAX

COURTESY JEFF FLAX

COURTESY MORRIS

*Glamorous looks for dressy or evening occasions. Note that contour and highlighting are used for these special looks only, and **very** carefully at that!*

COURTESY JEFF FLAX

Women over 40 often fear that they will look silly in makeup, but in fact, they look beautiful. Kathleen (left) is one of the most glamorous women we know with her soft pretty makeup and full white hair. Headwraps and touches of glitz (right), combined with makeup that is "all eyes and mouth," create grown-up-lady drama that makes being 40 fun!

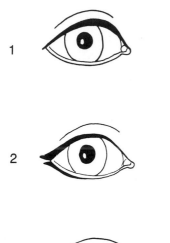

Eyeliner application (top to bottom): (1) for puffy eyelids; (2) for close-set eyes; (3) for all other eyes.

Shadow liner is used for contour in the crease, or it can be moistened and used as a soft powder liner.

Light Coloring	Medium Coloring	Dark Coloring
Gray	Sage green	Dark olive
Green-taupe	Brown	Dark brown
Slate blue	Dark plum	Dark emerald
Purple	Deep royal	Black

Pencil liners or liquid liners are used only at the lash line.

Light Coloring	Medium Coloring	Dark Coloring
Charcoal	Black	Black
Teal	Royal	Navy
Brown	Brown	

Mascara colors are more limited, making mascara the easiest makeup choice of all.

Light Coloring	Medium Coloring	Dark Coloring
Brown	Brown	Black
Charcoal	Black	Navy

BLUSH COLORS

Hue	Light Coloring	Medium Coloring	Dark Coloring
Earth rose	Bridal pink	Soft rose	Deep rose
Coral rose	Soft coral	Beige-coral	Bright coral
Pink rose	Mauve	Old rose	Fuchsia
Tea rose	Buff pink	Tea rose	Deep tea rose
Frost	Mauve frost	Rose frost	Deep pink frost
Contour	Light	Medium	Medium

YOUR MAKEUP COLORS

Choosing makeup products can be overwhelming and confusing when you are confronted with thousands of products. For that reason it is important to remember from time to time which products you have tried and liked. Fill out the chart above as you discover your favorites and use it as a guide when shopping for refills.

PERSONAL COLOR AND BRAND CHART

	Color	Product	Tool
Concealer	_____	_____	Cotton swabs
Foundation	_____	_____	Cosmetic sponge
Translucent powder	_____	_____	Powder brush
Blush	_____	_____	Blush brush
Contour (optional)	_____	_____	Contour brush
Eyebrows	_____	_____	Brow brush
Medium shadow	_____	_____	Shadow sponge applicator or fluff brush
Light shadow or highlighter	_____	_____	
Shadow liner (optional)	_____	_____	
Pencil liner	_____	_____	
Liquid eyeliner (optional)	_____	_____	
Mascara	_____	_____	Lash comb/brush
Lip liner	_____	_____	
Lipstick	_____	_____	Lip brush
Lip gloss	_____	_____	

REMINDER

Putting on your makeup (and fixing your hair) is *not* optional. Good grooming is for every day—the day you don't is the day you run into everyone you know, including the man you didn't marry in high school!

13

Professional Grooming and Model Tips

EXQUISITE GOOD GROOMING, in my opinion, is not an option to be saved for state occasions. It is a mandate for every day because it shows pride in your person and projects a cared-for image that others react to positively.

There are grooming functions that must be performed daily and those that can be done twice a year. It is necessary, however for the totally well-groomed woman to organize her grooming schedule and tools as she organizes her closet and drawers. Proper grooming should become second nature to a woman, something without which she feels naked.

The vice president of Big Beauties/Little Women, Virginia DeBerry, says that women over 30 seem to do one of two things where grooming is concerned: give up or fight like mad. Unfortunately, I think she is right. Virginia is a beautifully groomed woman who likes to spend her rare days off doing as little as possible, resting up for the next week of manic agency activity. She and I both agree that bliss is a Saturday spent goofing off until late afternoon when we mosey out to do the supermarket/dry cleaner/cobbler errands. Neither of us would dream of running those Saturday errands (Manhattanites do everything on Saturday) without neat hair and daytime makeup. Good grooming is too deeply ingrained for us to take a day off and feel right going out.

Very wealthy women can afford to spend a lot of time and money being pampered to beauty, but most of us have to rely on our own resources in the privacy of our own bathrooms. There, with any luck, you will arrange your grooming tools in an attractive way so that you enjoy this time you give to yourself. My models are a fountain of information and have been incredibly creative with their grooming tips and other useful ideas, so read carefully lest you miss a goodie.

NAILS, HANDS AND FEET

- If nails are very weak or brittle, consider having a professional weekly manicure until they are stronger.
- Apply night cream around your nails as on your face.
- Massage olive oil into nails on a regular basis to help strengthen them.
- Don't forget to clean under your fingernails regularly. Use a nail brush or a cotton swab dipped in remover.
- Soak discolored nails in a mixture of lemon juice and oil for a few minutes and then file *lightly*.
- If you do not know how to do a proper manicure or pedicure, treat yourself to one professional job and watch carefully.
- Keep hand cream by the side of the dish sink and use it often.
- If your hands and feet are rough, try this shock therapy. Once in bed (so you don't slide across your bedroom floor) put a disgusting amount of petroleum jelly on your hands and feet and sleep in white cotton gloves and socks.
- If your hands and feet are cracked or itchy in the winter, soak them for 5 minutes in cool tea and try the shock therapy treatment. This treatment helps control foot odor too.
- Put cologne on your feet and palms.
- Take care of toenails and calluses once a week for foot comfort. Rough, callused feet and jagged toenails are a turn-off.
- Silk or linen wraps, nail glue, nail tips and acrylic sculptured nails weaken your own nails and require weekly or biweekly maintenance—but they may be the salvation for problem nails. Once you start having these special manicures, you are (1) hooked on the wonderful way your hands look, and (2) forced to continue due to the damage to your natural nails.

Exquisite good grooming should be part of your routine every day—even on weekends. It affects the way you feel about yourself, which in turn affects how others react to you.
COURTESY RUSS

- Pale nails make your hands look longer.
- Short nails can be very chic, if nicely polished.
- A coat of clear polish each day will make a manicure last longer (until your nails are too thick to lift).
- Nails should never be more than 1/4-inch beyond the tip of your finger. Almost every man I know (and most women too) hate long, dragon-lady nails.
- Ill-kempt, cigarette-stained fingernails with ragged cuticles are slovenly.
- Neglected hands look old before their time.

HOW TO GIVE A MANICURE

1. Remove old polish.
2. Soak nails in warm water and dishwashing detergent.
3. Push cuticles back gently with fingers and baby oil or vegetable oil.
4. Shape nails with the soft side of an emery board.
5. Clip hang nails from the cuticles and reapply oil. ·
6. Rinse hands and massage generously with cream.
7. Apply base coat.
8. Apply two coats of polish.
9. Use an orange stick dipped in polish remover to clean up any polish on cuticles.
10. Apply top coat. Let dry 30 minutes

HOW TO GIVE A PEDICURE

Basically the same as a manicure, but after soaking feet, use a pumice stone to remove calluses. (I use a disposable razor *very gently* on bad calluses, and then use a pumice stone to smooth, also very gently. If you do this, be careful!)

SKIN

- Put white toothpaste on a pimple to help dry it up overnight.
- Rub the film from inside an eggshell on oily parts of your face (T-zone) and let dry for an instant mask.
- Apply eye cream gently with your fourth finger (the least strong, so the least pressure).
- Put moisturizer and night cream on your neck also.
- Stay out of the sun!

- Dip a cotton swab in milk of magnesia and rub on a blemish to take the redness out.
- Place cold cucumber slices on your eyelids to relieve tired eyes.
- Put baking soda and witch hazel in your bath and use a loofah. Afterward, rub on baby oil (wait until you get out of the tub—no broken legs please), and crawl into warm pajamas or sweats for an all-over body-beautiful treatment.
- Use cold witch hazel as a great summer freshener.
- Drink 8-10 glasses of water daily to moisturize from within.
- If you belong to a health club, try the steam bath. It's heaven for your skin.

MAKEUP

- Hair spray takes out lipstick stains.
- Concealer, loose powder, light blush, eyeshadow and lip gloss make a great natural daytime look.
- Gold eyeshadow applied to the entire lid with a 5/8″ wide brush is very glamorous.
- Blush brought close to the outer corners of your eyes tends to minimize dark circles.
- A dot of gold eyeshadow in the center of your upper and lower lips (over your lipstick) makes a glamorous evening look.
- Loose powder in peach or pink warms up a pale face.
- Powder eyeshadow over liquid eyeliner sets and softens the line.
- The buff-puff should be used on your mouth, too.
- Mineral water spritzed on finished makeup sets it.

HAIR

- To avoid dryness, dilute shampoo with water if you wash hair daily.
- Use baby oil or mayonnaise as a hair moisturizer. Leave on 1 hour and wash out.
- For very dry or dull hair, put olive oil in your hair and on your scalp. Massage and leave on hair wrapped in plastic wrap for 30 minutes. Wash hair.
- Use dishwashing liquid as shampoo once a month to strip away shampoo and spray buildup.

COURTESY ALCINDOR

COURTESY VICTOR POEDESSER

Women over 30 often fall into two categories of grooming: they either give up entirely or they pay more attention to it than ever. Both Ruth (top) and Liz (bottom) are two beautiful examples of the latter.

- Try a cool-water rinse to close up your scalp pores.
- For shine, use 2 tablespoons vinegar in 1 pint of water as a final rinse after shampooing (then rinse out the vinegar for your nose, please).
- Use a blow-dry protector spray before drying to prevent heat damage.
- Cover your hair in the sun. (What are you doing out in the sun?)
- Massage your night cream into your hair and sleep with a towel on your pillow. Wash out in the morning.

REMOVING UNWANTED HAIR

- Electrolysis is expensive and takes forever, but it is eventually permanent.
- Waxing hurts but is effective. Try wax strips and never wax the same area twice at the same time—use a tweezer to get any strays.
- For bleaching arms and legs, my mother taught me this: Mix 1 bottle hydrogen peroxide, 2-3 drops ammonia and white henna (available at drugstore) to make a paste. Leave on for 20 minutes, and rinse.
- To remove bikini hair: (Who needs a bikini anyway? I don't like bathing suits cut up to my waist—I think they're immodest and a bit much. I'll wax that sensitive part of my anatomy when I meet a man who would pay someone to tar and feather (cheesecloth) his groin—in short, never.) For a saner method, try a bikini electric shaver and an after-shave cooling cream (aloe) or an antibacterial cream. The rashes in this area are caused by skin that has been nicked at the top of the hair follicle.

BREATH AND TEETH

- Rub a paste of baking soda and hydrogen peroxide over your teeth and rinse with salt water to brighten your smile for a special occasion.
- Bad breath is caused by:
    - Illness
    - Stomach acid
    - Smoking
    - Garlic, gin, onions, cheese, milk, etc.

- ○ Improper brushing and dental care
- ○ Food particles between teeth.
- See your dentist, brush your teeth often (including your tongue) and try sprays, parsley and cloves for temporary bad breath.
- Bad-looking teeth are no longer necessary. These are the newest developments in cosmetic dentistry according to Dr. Jeff Golub of New York City.

> Cosmetic dentistry cost is about 50%-75% per tooth of the price of old-fashioned caps. There are two types of cosmetic dentistry, bonding and porcelain laminates, used today. You can estimate the number of teeth to be done by smiling in the mirror and counting the teeth that show (usually 6-10).

> *Bonding* is a reversible procedure in which a soft puttylike material is used to sculpt new teeth over old without marring the original teeth. Once hardened, bonded teeth may stain from smoking, coffee or red wine.

> *Porcelain laminates* are thin pieces of porcelain that are affixed to teeth that have been "prepped," causing some visual damage to the enamel of the original tooth. Porcelain laminates are quite chip- and stain-resistant and more expensive than bonding.

SCENTS

- Deodorants and antiperspirants are the obvious way to deal with underarm odor.
  - ○ If these products irritate your underarm skin, try using baking soda mixed with talc.
  - ○ If the combination of shaving and deodorants gives you a rash, try an electric shaver.
  - ○ If you develop an underarm rash, don't use deodorant until the rash clears. At least twice a day wash thoroughly and apply rubbing alcohol and an antibacterial cream.

- For persistent vaginal odors or irritations:
  - See your gynecologist.
  - Try a tampon dipped in yogurt (plain, no blueberry swirl or nuts and raisins, please). Many women swear by this pH-balancing procedure.
- For a special effect on a special evening, spray cologne on your light bulbs.
- If money is scarce, substitute hash oil for perfume. It's less expensive and very long-lasting.

EXERCISE

- Walk, it's the best activity.
- Try 5 or 10 minutes a day of exercise. It can do wonders for parts of you that need tone:
  - H's should try sidebends and partial sit-ups.
  - O's should try partial sit-ups and leg raises.
  - A's should try leg-ups and leg swings.
  - X's should go away (Oops, me jealous? Never!) or do arm circles and partial sit-ups.
- Use an exercise bike for 15 minutes a day while watching TV.
- For a good investment, hire a trainer once or twice to make a simple plan for you.

DIET

I'm no great dieter, in fact I usually gain weight when I try to diet, but I know that weight is a numbers game. If you give up 100 calories a day, you will lose 10 pounds a year. If you exercise more (walk 10 extra blocks a day), you'll also lose 10 pounds in a year. That's 20 pounds so you can have pizza for lunch! It's an input/output trade-off, so unless you're willing to make some major changes on a permanent basis, forget it—dieting doesn't work. Only permanent changes of eating habits work, and for many of us that's nigh on to impossible.

Most of the sane people I know concern themselves with proper nutrition—three meals balanced from the food groups. They do not worry about either extreme of dieting or emotional eating (pasta doesn't cure PMS?). If you think you have any eating disorder, please get help.

Professional treatment works, and you will be amazed to see how much company you have out there.

Some easy permanent changes guaranteed to cut weight are:
- Cut fats to 20-30% of your total calories. Your heart will thank you.
- Cut white sugar intake to nil. You don't need it, and it can cause emotional problems.
- Cut liquor to an occasional wine spritzer. Not only does alcohol have calories, but hangovers set off binges.
- Collect low-fat, delicious recipes. I have about ten of them and they are great! (So why aren't I thin? I am down to five meals a day!)
- Try a vitamin and 10 minutes of exercises in the morning instead of coffee. Caffeine stimulates the appetite.
- *Never* skip breakfast—you'll make up for it by 10 p.m. when you should be looking for your children.
- Eat a sane meal (like Scarlett O'Hara) before you go out to a big tempting party.

PICK-ME-UP

After lunch and late in the afternoon, give yourself a "500-mile checkup" for beauty and morale.
- Brush teeth.
- Mop up runny eye makeup.
- Powder nose.
- Reapply lipstick.
- Spritz perfume.
- Brush hair.
- Do 10 jumping jacks—it's better than a cup of coffee for energy.

ILLUSIONS OF HEIGHT

If you are short and wish to look taller, *do* wear:
- V-necks
- Vertical lines (dress/button plackets)
- Vertical accessories (beads, long scarves)
- Monochromatic outfits

- Pared-down forms and no excessive fullness (floats, poet sleeves)
- Delicate fabrics
- Hose and shoes matched to hem color
- Short jackets
- Moderate-height heels
- Longer skirts (with a heel of 1½ to 2½ inches)
- Tunics and pants.

To avoid visually shortening your line, *don't* wear:

- Turtlenecks or other high necks
- Excessively full fabrics
- Heavy textures
- Big plaids or prints
- Massive color/contrast clothing "blocks"
- Long jackets (below the hip) with short skirts
- Extremely high heels
- Wide belts
- Big handbags
- Horizontal lines

Remember, you are what you are. Don't try to be 6 feet tall—just keep proportion in mind. Wear skirts any length you wish, but keep your eyes open and watch what you wear with a given length.

8-DAY MIRACLE GROOMING PLAN

DAY 1—Organize your grooming tools and bathroom cosmetics in straw baskets, pretty jars or clear plastic containers. Make a "need to buy" list.

DAY 2—Go shopping for supplies. Do an at-home facial.

DAY 3—Try a new makeup. Soak in the tub. Push back your cuticles after your bath. Shave (legs, underarms, bikini) with sudsy shaving cream or an electric shaver after your bath. Slather yourself with baby oil before bed.

DAY 4—Make an appointment and have a professional manicure and pedicure. Watch what they do so you can learn to do it yourself. Walk for 10-15 minutes—take Fido.

DAY 5—See a hairdresser. Have a consultation first, then go for the works.

DAY 6—Take a long bath. Moisturize your skin again from head to toe. See your dentist.

DAY 7—Do another at-home facial, and moisturize your face. Do 10 minutes on an exercise bike and 5 minutes of exercises just for your body type (see Exercise, page 214).

DAY 8—Get up dedicated to an entire day of not being on a diet. Experiment with blow-drying your hair with mousse. Go shopping at lunch time or have lunch with a friend. Walk 10 blocks (exercise is not inconsistent with a no-diet posture). Start or end this day with a lovely bath to relax. Try repeating the best part of this week, forever. You deserve it.

GROOMING TIMETABLE

WHAT	HOW OFTEN	WHAT	HOW OFTEN
Skin		*Hair*	
Cleanse	Twice a day	Wash	Every 1 or 2 days
Freshen	Twice a day	Condition	Every 1 or 2 days
Moisturize	Twice a day	Color	Every 4-8 weeks
Facial	Once a week	Perm	Every 4-6 months
Nails and hands		Moisturize	Once a week
Manicure	Once a week	*Superfluous hair*	
Pedicure	Once a month	Electrolysis	Twice a month
Moisturize	Once a day	Waxing	Every 6 weeks
Makeup		Depilatory	Once a week
Day makeup	7 days a week	Shaving	Every 2-4 days
Special occasion	As needed	Bleaching	Every 3 weeks
Teeth		Bikini shave	Once a week
Dentist (cleaning)	Twice a year	*Exercise and diet*	
Brushing	After meals	Walk	Once a day
Flossing	After meals	Bike/at home/health club	Three times a week
Mouthwash	After brushing	Vitamins	Once a day
Bathing		Good nutrition	Every day
Bath/shower	Once a day		
Douche	Ask your gynecologist		
Deodorant/powder	Once a day		

TURN-OFFS AND TURN-ONS

Men and women are usually quite interested in the opinion of the opposite sex, so just for fun, we asked many of the men and women we know for a list of the major turn-offs and turn-ons. Measure yourself and add to them, or if you're really brave, ask your man his opinion—that could be enlightening.

For fun, I asked ten men and ten women to list what they find most attractive and unattractive in the opposite sex. Review this list and see what you can add. Make note of any turn-offs of which you might be guilty.

UNISEX TURN-OFFS		UNISEX TURN-ONS	
Wandering eyes	Sulkiness	Sensitivity	Cheerfulness
Bad breath	Envy	Humor	Positiveness
Body odor	Bragging	Confidence	Cleanliness
Dirty nails	Name-dropping	Listening	Strong interests
Negativity	Lying about age or	Warmth	Nice hands
Jealousy	weight	Smiles	Graceful carriage
Selfishness	Drinking too much	Laughter	Good grooming
Loudness	Drugs	Sincerity	Friendliness
Foul language	Dirty hair	Intelligence	Loyalty
Undue anger/temper	Crude voice or accent	Honesty	Poise

TURN-OFFS FOR WOMEN		TURN-ONS FOR WOMEN	
Self-consciousness	Beer belly	Masculinity	Voice
Macho behavior	Extreme vanity	Protectiveness	Knowing how to fix
Aggressiveness	Jewelry	Supportiveness	things
Messiness	Open shirts	Consistency	Making dinner for her
Nervousness	Crudeness	Romance	Calling frequently
Preoccupation with	Sexual gestures	Tactile sense	Being able to cry
women's looks	Euphemisms	Hand-holding	Commenting when she
Critical nature	Talking to cleavage	Little things: a card, a	looks nice
Toupees		flower, an article	Liking her cooking
Cigars		from the paper	Letting her baby him
Beer breath		Dignity	when he's sick

Beautiful eyes and a sense of humor are mentioned often when men are asked what they find most attractive in a woman.

COURTESY JEFF FLAX

COURTESY JEFF FLAX

COURTESY JEFF FLAX

TURN-OFFS FOR MEN		TURN-ONS FOR MEN	
Militant feminism	Malicious gossip	Likes kids and animals	Soft hands
Dressing mannishly	Ungainly walk	Likes men	Perfume
Not dressing or acting one's age	Empty fridge	Likes being a woman	Legs
	Chewing gum	Thoughtfulness, tact	High heels
Excessive neatness	"Buy me/take me/show me" attitude	Rationality	Dresses nicely
Playing dumb or feigned helplessness	Too much cleavage	Respectfulness to others	Sweetness
Dirty lingerie	Very long nails	Humility	Soft voice
Perspiration stains	Talking about other men	Intelligence	Restraint
Heavy, obvious or bad makeup job	Vanity	Dresses up at night	
Gold-digging	Hypochondria	Sense of humor	
Non-stop chatter	Contrived cuteness	Slight bawdiness	
		Eyes	
		Mouth	

Note how many of the turn-offs/turn-ons have to do with courtesy and grooming. Enough said?

COURTESY SONNY BACK

Christine with a model's best friend—the camera. Whatever your body shape, you can learn to pose at flattering angles.

H-O-A-X CAMERA POSES

Before you think we have forgotten completely about the H-O-A-X Formula (although all the above tips are provided to help you with your "presentation"), let's discuss what my models have learned about being photographed to best advantage. Models are paid up to $2,000 a day for learning to do these things by instinct. There are many ways to take a nice picture, but practicing grace and good H-O-A-X common sense is the best place to start.

- Stand up straight. Imagine that someone is pulling a hair up from the top of your head. This is the way you should stand and walk.
- Keep your hands slightly curved for grace.
- Practice graceful poses with your feet and legs—slightly apart but not too much (or you will look like you have just joined the Hell's Angels).
- Keep your face on an even plane with the camera lens. If your head is too high, you'll look double-chinny. If it is too low, you'll look like your nose is in love with your chin.
- Look directly into the lens and think warm thoughts. Think of something you love. I think of puppies and kittens, or of Fooey, my shih-tzu.
- If you look away from the camera for drama, focus on a thought or an object—blank stares aren't dramatic.
- H: Put one hand, fingers forward, at your waist to make it appear to indent. Turn your body at a three-quarter angle to the camera.
- O: Pull in your midsection and do not lean against anything. Leaning can push your tummy or breasts out into an unflattering pose.
- A: Do not push either hip out, but turn your hips at a three-quarter angle to the camera and turn your torso slightly back to the camera.
- X: Do not "profile" your bosom. Turn your entire torso straight on and do not confuse standing up straight with sticking out your breasts. Go for a soft, feminine pose.
- Say "cheese." Click!

14 | *Planning and Organizing Your Wardrobe*

MANY OF THE BEST-DRESSED women I know have shared the same surprising wardrobe tip: they learned to dress well at a time when they were on a very strict budget. Lack of funds motivated these clever women to learn to be both shrewd and selective in their limited choices of new garments and accessories.

The first step in planning and building a wardrobe is to assess what you have—both in your current closet and in you, yourself. Change is never easy, but if you have the desire for personal image improvement, you will want to tackle this project with enthusiasm. With proper wardrobe planning, you will find the fulfillment of all the work you have done to date.

Try to be objective and to imagine that you are a professional wardrobe planner/image consultant whom you have engaged to "redo" you.

REVIEW THE BASICS

The first step is to review everything you have been learning in this book:

My body type: _____

My best colors: _____

_____

_____

_____

_____

My favorite styles: _____

_____

_____

My lifestyle needs (percentage of time spent):

At work _____

At home _____

At leisure _____

At dressy functions _____

EXAMINE YOUR CLOSET

Set aside an evening for the following steps:

1. Go through your closet and arrange this season's clothes in the following order. Then do the same for next season's clothes (if they are in the same closet):
   - Dressy clothes
   - Daytime dresses
   - Suits
   - Blouses
   - Sweaters
   - Pants
   - Shirts
   - Leisure clothes (jogging suits, very casual items)
   - Hanging lingerie (I hang up slips and nightgowns. They stay neater.)
   - Slips
   - Half slips, camisoles
   - Robes
   - Gowns
   - Coats

2. Remove from your closet any item which is:
   - Worn or in a state of disrepair
   - Too small or too big
   - Blatantly out of date
   - All wrong for you in terms of color, form or line, or style.

3. Do with all of these items as you will, but I recommend that you mend or alter, if possible, those in the first two categories, and discard (yard sale, Salvation Army, etc.) the rest.

MAKE A LIST

List the remaining clothes by category as shown on the following charts. Include notes on what you need (navy pants for that red blouse, etc.).

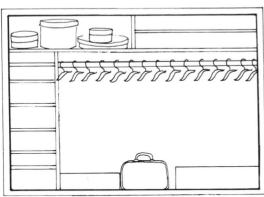

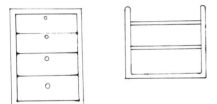

Organizing your closet contents is essential before you can assess your wardrobe needs.

WINTER WARDROBE CHART
LEISURE / HOME

Item	Color	Purpose	Accessories
Winter Activewear:			
Winter Pants/Jeans:			
Winter Tops (Sweaters, Vests, Blouses):			

WORK / DAYTIME

Item	*Color*	*Purpose*	*Accessories*

Winter Dresses:

_____ _____ _____ _____
_____ _____ _____ _____
_____ _____ _____ _____
_____ _____ _____ _____
_____ _____ _____ _____

Winter Suits:

_____ _____ _____ _____
_____ _____ _____ _____
_____ _____ _____ _____

Winter Slacks:

_____ _____ _____ _____
_____ _____ _____ _____
_____ _____ _____ _____

Winter Skirts:

_____ _____ _____ _____
_____ _____ _____ _____
_____ _____ _____ _____

Winter Blouses:

_____ _____ _____ _____
_____ _____ _____ _____
_____ _____ _____ _____
_____ _____ _____ _____

Winter Jackets/Vests/Sweaters:

_____ _____ _____ _____
_____ _____ _____ _____
_____ _____ _____ _____
_____ _____ _____ _____
_____ _____ _____ _____

DRESSY

Item	*Color*	*Purpose*	*Accessories*

Winter Gowns/Dresses:

_____ _____ _____ _____
_____ _____ _____ _____
_____ _____ _____ _____

Winter Tops:

_____ _____ _____ _____
_____ _____ _____ _____
_____ _____ _____ _____
_____ _____ _____ _____
_____ _____ _____ _____
_____ _____ _____ _____
_____ _____ _____ _____

Winter Pants/Skirts:

_____ _____ _____ _____
_____ _____ _____ _____
_____ _____ _____ _____

LINGERIE

Winter Slips/Half Slips:

_____ _____ _____ _____
_____ _____ _____ _____
_____ _____ _____ _____
_____ _____ _____ _____

Winter Camisoles:

_____ _____ _____ _____
_____ _____ _____ _____

Winter Nightgowns:

_____ _____ _____ _____
_____ _____ _____ _____
_____ _____ _____ _____
_____ _____ _____ _____

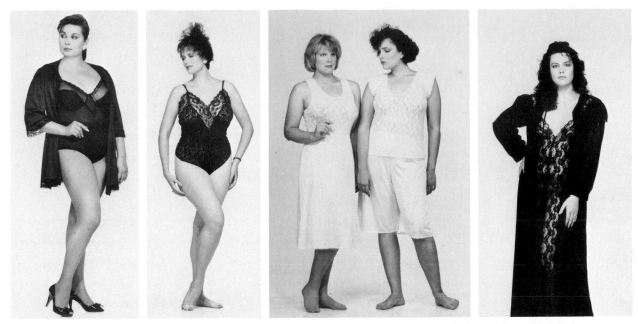

Lingerie: Basics can be pretty, and pretty should be basic (from left): (1) A body briefer, which is better for H Deborah than a bra and girdle (O's also swear by this garment). (2) The lacy teddy is sexy and feminine on X Tara. (3) The one-piece slip (excellent under clingy garments) and the shoulder pad T-shirt with a split petticoat flatter all body types. (4) Every woman should own a peignoir set like this lace panel gown and Victorian robe.

Winter Robes:

_____ _____ _____ _____
_____ _____ _____ _____
_____ _____ _____ _____
_____ _____ _____ _____
_____ _____ _____ _____
_____ _____ _____ _____
_____ _____ _____ _____

Winter Loungewear:

_____ _____ _____ _____
_____ _____ _____ _____
_____ _____ _____ _____
_____ _____ _____ _____
_____ _____ _____ _____
_____ _____ _____ _____
_____ _____ _____ _____
_____ _____ _____ _____

OUTERWEAR

Item	Color	Purpose	Accessories
Winter Coats:			
_____	_____	_____	_____
_____	_____	_____	_____
_____	_____	_____	_____
_____	_____	_____	_____
_____	_____	_____	_____
Winter Raincoats:			
_____	_____	_____	_____
_____	_____	_____	_____
_____	_____	_____	_____

SUMMER WARDROBE CHART
LEISURE / HOME

Item	Color	Purpose	Accessories
Swimsuits:			
_____	_____	_____	_____
_____	_____	_____	_____
Cover-ups:			
_____	_____	_____	_____
_____	_____	_____	_____
Summer Shorts:			
_____	_____	_____	_____
_____	_____	_____	_____
_____	_____	_____	_____
Other Summer Activewear:			
_____	_____	_____	_____
_____	_____	_____	_____
_____	_____	_____	_____

Item	*Color*	*Purpose*	*Accessories*

Summer Pants:

_____ _____ _____ _____

_____ _____ _____ _____

_____ _____ _____ _____

_____ _____ _____ _____

_____ _____ _____ _____

Summer Skirts:

_____ _____ _____ _____

_____ _____ _____ _____

_____ _____ _____ _____

_____ _____ _____ _____

_____ _____ _____ _____

Summer Tops:

_____ _____ _____ _____

_____ _____ _____ _____

_____ _____ _____ _____

_____ _____ _____ _____

_____ _____ _____ _____

_____ _____ _____ _____

WORK / DAYTIME

Summer Dresses:

_____ _____ _____ _____

_____ _____ _____ _____

_____ _____ _____ _____

_____ _____ _____ _____

_____ _____ _____ _____

_____ _____ _____ _____

_____ _____ _____ _____

_____ _____ _____ _____

_____ _____ _____ _____

_____ _____ _____ _____

_____ _____ _____ _____

Item	Color	Purpose	Accessories

Summer Suits:

_____

Summer Slacks:

_____

Summer Skirts:

_____

Summer Blouses:

_____

Summer Jackets/Sweaters:

_____

Summer Raincoats:

_____

DRESSY

Item	Color	Purpose	Accessories
Summer Gowns/Dresses:			
_____	_____	_____	_____
_____	_____	_____	_____
_____	_____	_____	_____
_____	_____	_____	_____
Summer Pants/Skirts:			
_____	_____	_____	_____
_____	_____	_____	_____
_____	_____	_____	_____
_____	_____	_____	_____
Summer Tops:			
_____	_____	_____	_____
_____	_____	_____	_____
_____	_____	_____	_____
_____	_____	_____	_____
_____	_____	_____	_____
_____	_____	_____	_____
_____	_____	_____	_____
_____	_____	_____	_____
_____	_____	_____	_____

Organize your accessories by type and season (clear plastic boxes are great):

Summer (Color)	*Summer (Color)*	*Winter (Color)*	*Winter (Color)*
Shoes			
_____	_____	_____	_____
_____	_____	_____	_____
_____	_____	_____	_____
_____	_____	_____	_____
_____	_____	_____	_____
_____	_____	_____	_____
_____	_____	_____	_____
_____	_____	_____	_____
_____	_____	_____	_____
_____	_____	_____	_____

Summer (Color)	*Summer (Color)*	*Winter (Color)*	*Winter (Color)*

Boots

_____	_____	_____	_____
_____	_____	_____	_____

Gloves

_____	_____	_____	_____
_____	_____	_____	_____

Handbags

_____	_____	_____	_____
_____	_____	_____	_____
_____	_____	_____	_____
_____	_____	_____	_____
_____	_____	_____	_____

Scarves

_____	_____	_____	_____
_____	_____	_____	_____
_____	_____	_____	_____
_____	_____	_____	_____
_____	_____	_____	_____
_____	_____	_____	_____

Hats

_____	_____	_____	_____
_____	_____	_____	_____

Belts

_____	_____	_____	_____
_____	_____	_____	_____
_____	_____	_____	_____
_____	_____	_____	_____

JEWELRY (NO SEASON)

Necklaces

_____   _____
_____   _____
_____   _____
_____   _____
_____   _____
_____   _____
_____   _____
_____   _____

Earrings

_____   _____
_____   _____
_____   _____
_____   _____
_____   _____
_____   _____
_____   _____
_____   _____
_____   _____
_____   _____
_____   _____

Bracelets

_____   _____
_____   _____
_____   _____
_____   _____

Pins

_____   _____
_____   _____
_____   _____
_____   _____
_____   _____

LINGERIE DRAWERS

List color and number of the following:

Shoulder Pads

_____   _____
_____   _____
_____   _____

Bras

_____   _____
_____   _____
_____   _____
_____   _____

Panties

_____   _____
_____   _____
_____   _____
_____   _____
_____   _____

Body Briefers

_____   _____
_____   _____

Girdles

_____   _____
_____   _____

Hosiery

_____   _____
_____   _____
_____   _____
_____   _____
_____   _____
_____   _____

EVALUATE YOUR WARDROBE

Evaluate your wardrobe by category. In which categories are you generally in need?

	Summer	*Winter*
Leisure clothes	_____	_____
Work clothes	_____	_____
Daytime clothes	_____	_____
Dressy clothes*	_____	_____

*Don't forget the all-important category, dressy casual: silk shirts, velvet slacks, etc.

SPECIFIC NEEDS

Summer   *Winter*

Dresses

_____   _____
_____   _____
_____   _____
_____   _____
_____   _____

Suits

_____   _____
_____   _____

Tops

_____   _____
_____   _____
_____   _____
_____   _____
_____   _____

Pants

_____   _____
_____   _____
_____   _____
_____   _____

Summer

Skirts

_____

_____

_____

_____

Jackets

_____

_____

_____

_____

Coats

_____

_____

Shoes

_____

_____

_____

_____

Hosiery

_____

_____

_____

_____

Lingerie

_____

_____

_____

_____

_____

Accessories

_____

_____

_____

_____

_____

Winter

_____

_____

_____

_____

_____

_____

_____

_____

_____

_____

_____

_____

_____

_____

_____

_____

_____

_____

_____

_____

_____

_____

_____

_____

_____

Remember, any future purchases you make must be:
- Correctly sized
- Flattering in color
- Flattering in silhouette
- In keeping with your style choices
- Coordinated with other items (accessories, coats, separates in your closet)
- Something you love.

ORGANIZE YOUR GROOMING TOOLS

Organize your bathroom with your grooming tools:
- Makeup
- Hair-care products
- Skin-care products
- Fragrance
- Grooming aids (out of sight)
- Personal hygiene (out of sight)

Make a list of the grooming tools you need. Don't expect to buy them all at once; it will take time.

_____   _____

_____   _____

_____   _____

_____   _____

TIPS ON SHOPPING

If you were to ask what is my favorite leisure sport, I'd have to say "shopping, of course." I've seen T-shirts that say such things as:

"Born to shop"

"I shop, therefore I am."

"When things get tough, the tough go shopping."

When I have a minute, I'm going to go shopping for one of them (oversized and with shoulder pads because I'm an O).

Shopping is one of life's necessities, so why not enjoy it? If you have completed the wardrobe plan chart, you are already on your way to being a successful shopper because you have studied what you have in your current wardrobe, and made notes of what you need to augment it. Here are some tips to further simplify shopping:

- Try making a master list of what you need by color, season, price range and priority. Keep this list in your wallet.
- Plan to shop when you're not in a hurry and when you are in a good mood.
- Decide on the appropriate retail outlets.
- For any given item, choose several alternate styles and try them on to see which is most flattering.
- If you have consistent problems with fit, you probably should have clothes altered so they are right for your body. Skirts that "hike" or pants that "smile" or drag on the floor look sloppy. Do whatever is necessary for proper fit.
- Comparison-shop and watch for special sales, thus stretching your wardrobe dollar.
- When you buy an item, keep the receipt and leave the tags on. If you haven't worn the item in 10 days, think about returning it. Do you really need it? If you return it, do so immediately—be fair to the store.
- Carry a tape measure. If you're in a hurry and don't have time to try on a garment before buying it, measure the garment at its more fitted areas to see if it will fit your measurements. Hips and bust should measure your measurement plus 3 inches for ease. Try the garment on at home—I bet it will fit—this method never fails me.
- If you impulse-shop and run up a big bill that causes you undue anxiety, try on your purchases at home. Decide if you really need or want each of your purchases and return anything that doesn't "ring your bell" in the clear, calm light of your own boudoir.
- Catalog merchandise is also returnable, so don't hesitate to buy something by mail or phone for fear that you might be stuck with a lemon.
- Learn the names of brands that flatter and fit you well.
- Buy lingerie and hose on special sales and in quantity. If you have trouble finding your size, ask a store buyer to special order for you. When I find a body briefer that I like, I cut out the tag and style number (before washing obliterates it).
- Most of all, have fun with your shopping. Be our own Barbie doll and "dress *you* up."

COURTESY JEFF FLAX

Furrier Daniel Antonovich loves to see women looking beautiful. He believes fur can work on all body types.

HOW TO CHOOSE A FLATTERING FUR

Many large or short women want to wear fur but think they will look like a porcupine in mating season. In truth, long-haired furs often do add bulk to bulk and are for the taller woman who is slim to average in size. But all women can wear fur if they choose.

New York furrier Daniel Antonovich gave me the following tips. He says, "You can *like* a cloth coat, but you should *love* a fur. Buying fur is both romantic and traumatic—romantic, because you know how glamorous you are going to look, and traumatic because you are parting with a lot of money."

Fur is a long-term investment, so choose carefully. Look for striping that is not too broad, generous fur facing (the fur turned to the inside at the edge) and an ample fit. In choosing a fur color, remember that dark is recessive to the eye and that light is expansive. For specific **H-O-A-X** body types, consider the following:

- **H:** Try straight cuts and avoid belted styles and styles with too much fullness below the waist.
- **O:** Try edge-to-edge closings and low break lines (closures), and avoid belts and thick fur collars.
- **A:** Try traditional A-line, full-sweep cuts. You are ideal for fur, but avoid narrow coats.
- **X:** Try simple, semishaped cuts with full sweeps, and avoid high-cut collar treatments.

Furs that are good for average and above-average-sized women are mink, sheared beaver, nutria, fitch and low-nap fox.

CAPSULE WARDROBING AND SOFT DRESSING

A *capsule wardrobe* is one built on five to eight pieces in a two-color scheme that can be mixed and matched to make many outfits.

Soft dressing refers to the use of clothes that are usually unlined, unstructured (interfaced) and of cut and fabric that is designed to drape softly.

An ideal way to build a wardrobe is to choose two

colors and purchase a capsule wardrobe of soft pieces to mix and match. Over a few seasons you will acquire quite the wardrobe.

HOW TO "CAPSULE" WITH SOFT DRESSING

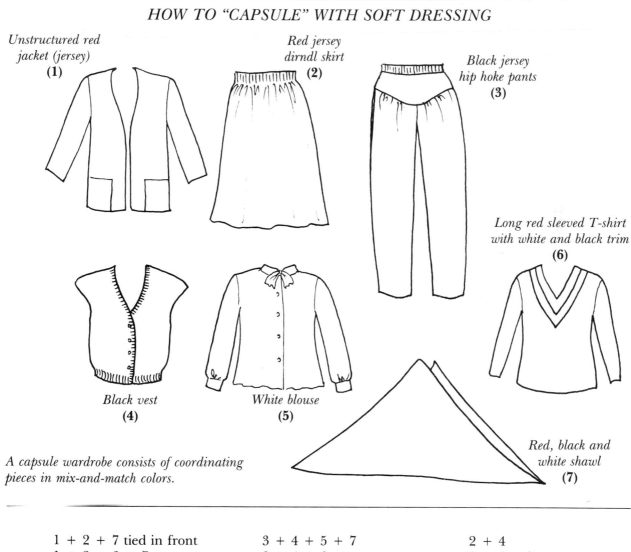

Unstructured red jacket (jersey)
(1)

Red jersey dirndl skirt
(2)

Black jersey hip hoke pants
(3)

Long red sleeved T-shirt with white and black trim
(6)

Black vest
(4)

White blouse
(5)

Red, black and white shawl
(7)

A capsule wardrobe consists of coordinating pieces in mix-and-match colors.

1 + 2 + 7 tied in front	3 + 4 + 5 + 7	2 + 4
1 + 2 + 6 + 7	3 + 4 + 6	2 + 6 + 7
1 + 3 + 5 + 7	3 + 6	1 + 2 + 7 worn as halter
1 + 2 + 5 + 7	3 + 7 worn as halter	1 + 3 + 7 worn as halter
1 + 3 + 6 + 7	2 + 6 + 7	2 + 4 + 1 + 7
3 + 5	3 + 6 + 7	2 + 4 + 1
1 + 2 + 5	3 + 4	2 + 6
1 + 2 + 6	3 + 4 + 7 over hip	2 + 6 + 4
1 + 3 + 7 tied in front	2 + 5	2 + 6 + 1
3 + 4 + 5	2 + 5 + 4	
3 + 4 + 6 + 7		*Et cetera, ad infinitum*

Planning a travel wardrobe is much easier when you pack tops and bottoms that can be interchanged.

PACKING AND TRAVEL

Travel is hard work, whether business or vacation. Here are some tips to make it easier.

- Pick outifts that interchange.
- Pick coordinating shoes, accessories and lingerie, and pack them in a separate accessory bag to go inside your suitcase (makes packing and unpacking easier).
- If you travel a lot, keep a permanent cosmetics/grooming bag packed to put in your suitcase. These little things take longer to pack and unpack than anything else.
- Do not travel with expensive jewelry in your suitcase. I have twice had my suitcase run over by loading trucks and the airlines did *not* cover the mangled gold jewelry.
- Organize your handbag so it is as light as possible.
- Organize your cosmetic bag with the following in a small zippered purse:

○ Small scissors	○ Compact with powder
○ Tweezers	○ Small blush and brush
○ Breath spray	○ Lipstick
○ Perfume (a sample is good)	○ Eyeliner pencil
○ Emery board	○ Mascara
○ Moisturizer (small sample)	○ Eyebrow pencil
○ Makeup base (small sample)	

- Wear comfortable but ladylike clothes for travel. An airline employee in Phoenix once told me that he had stopped a woman trying to board a plane in a bikini—and barefoot!
- If you're going to an unfamiliar city, ask how people dress there.
- Read the national weather report in *USA Today* or call long distance and get the weather report.
- Remove old destination tags from your luggage. Misery is you in Houston and your luggage in Atlanta.
- Don't overpack suitcases. Clothes will wrinkle more, and you increase the chances that luggage locks will burst.
- Bon voyage!

15

Golden Rules of the H-O-A-X Formula

You are what you are.

Your height, age and coloring are constant. What's more, statistics say that your weight and size are quite likely to remain the same. (Of all people who attempt to diet, only 3-5% actually lose weight and keep it off. 95-97% do not.) So make up your mind to deal with what and who you are in the most positive way and to *never* apologize to anyone for being you.

Comparing yourself to movie stars and models is self-defeating and unrealistic. Movie stars and models are usually the most perfect physical specimens of the current crop (and are often tragically discarded when perfection fades or a new crop comes along). Further, they are dieted, exercised, made up, coiffured, groomed, dressed, lit and photographed to the nines—sometimes they are even photographed through pink gauze and retouched. This is not to be envied or confused with real life, as such extreme routines can be tedious and make one vain.

There is nothing uniquely "weird" about your body.

Believing that your body is odd is the ultimate HOAX. Many a woman seems to think that she alone has figure problems, and that they are some awful flaw or her fault. In fact, your body shape is hereditary. *The average woman is about 5'4" tall, weighs 143 pounds and is 32 years old.* If you are between 16 and 65 years old, wear a size 6 to 26 and are 5'0" to 6'0" tall, you fall into a category called "the vast overwhelming majority of women." Bemoaning your precise positioning will get you nowhere. Work with what you've got. Be proudly young, middle-aged, old, short, medium, tall, small, average or large.

> **The most important secret to looking good is dressing your shape properly.**

Whichever H-O-A-X type you are, dress it properly. When buying new clothes, choose from your many "best" silhouettes. The mistakes in your closet will be nil if you apply sound H-O-A-X principles of form, line, color and texture. Knowing how these elements can work for you is called "good taste."

Any time you are tempted to buy an exception to your best rules ask the advice of an honest friend. Dressing with the rules and not making a lot of exceptions until you know your best looks well reminds me of a Picasso quote. He said that he could not be an abstract painter until he was first an expert traditional painter. Basics first.

> **The best accessory is a three-way mirror.**

After all is said and done, you need to look at yourself from all angles and admire the results of your efforts. Is anything wrong? If so, change it. Knowing you look your best will flavor your entire day. Being comfortable with your clothes, accessories, hair and makeup will give you the ease and assured feeling to get on with your life.

> **Style is knowing how to project the real you to others.**

Style is a synonym for personal flair. It is also packaging and presentation. Having style enables you to put your unique signature on everything you do, say and wear. Versatility in your style self-image further enables you to have some fun with your clothes. Good taste comes from knowing rules—style comes from knowing you. Planning a wardrobe that reflects your sense of style (and personal good taste) is time-consuming, but totally necessary.

Mary with some of her models' photos.
COURTESY MICHAEL IAN

Planning and organization facilitate the daily "get it together" routine.

> *Accessories, hair and makeup can better balance your body shape and enhance your personal style.*

Flattering hair and makeup and eye-catching accessories are the best friends of the woman who wants to accentuate the positive and eliminate the negative. Pay careful attention to these elements because they are part of your total "presentation." Hair, makeup and accessories give you the means to call attention to your best features, in keeping with the advice of model Liz Dillon, "Distract, don't disguise."

> *Your looks are not the most important thing about you,*
> *but they greatly affect first impressions.*

Although your looks are not your most important characteristic, looking and feeling as good as you can does make you more attractive to people at first impression.

My college roommate once said that we *like* people for those things that seem wonderful about them at first, but we grow to *love* them for their rough edges. Put another way, people can only love us when they really get to know us—good and bad (great sense of humor and midriff bulge, for instance).

Even in romance, I see men and women in quite a flap over something they think is love, but which is in fact infatuation. A sure sign of infatuation is the inevitable googly-eyed statement, "He/She is the most perfectly wonderful person who ever lived." Later in a relationship, when reality and friendship kick in, perceived perfection fades and real love can begin to grow.

What does all this have to do with your appearance? Plenty! Dedicate yourself to looking your best for all the possible "first impressions" of your life, and watch the improvement in the way people react to you. They will later come to know who you really are and what "counts" to you—the most important parts of you.

> *Continued growth and self-knowledge*
> *require periodic inventories.*

I hope this book has served as a personal inventory for you and that you will repeat the sections you found most helpful. Personal inventories must be more than evaluations of your physical positive and negative traits, closet contents, style and lifestyle needs. They also need to be evaluations of your goals, priorities, inner needs and personality traits.

Many women put themselves down by thinking that any self-absorption is vain and selfish. In truth, no one is going to lead you down the paths of truth and fulfillment. You have to find your own way in life, ideally with the love and support of others. If you are sure of who you are, what you think and what counts to you, you are better able to serve your own needs and the needs of others. Take private time for periodic personal inventories—inside and out.

If life hands you a lemon, make lemonade.

There is some value in almost all of life's experiences. Keep positive and remain eternally optimistic. Such spirit shows on people (as does negativity) and draws people to you. In turn, others will bring answers and comfort at the worst of moments. Look for the good in all things, including yourself.

As women, we sell ourselves short when we try to fit into someone else's image of what we should be. I could scream with frustration when I think of all the time I have wasted trying to squeeze into a cookie-cutter image of perfect womanhood. The scream gets louder still when I think of other women's stories, including:

- The woman who told me she hadn't gone out with her husband for 4 years because she was ashamed of her 30-pound weight gain.
- The angry mother whose 15-year-old daughter was reduced to tears by a doctor who, while supposedly treating a strep throat, lectured her on her moderate overweight. He told her she'd never have any friends or boyfriends.
- The five-star southern beauty who told me she'd been divorced twice by men who couldn't deal with her weight. She was 5'8" and a size 12 who'd been an 8.
- The New England woman whose husband had asked her, "When are you going to lose that ugly fat?" She responded, "As soon as you move out."
- The California girl whose beau said he'd marry her if she'd lose 5 pounds. She did. He married someone else.

- The confused Massachusetts woman who went to a clinic and lost 75 pounds, and 6 months later went into therapy because she said angrily, "I'm still me. Why did I have to go through this to be liked?"
- The woman who told me after a show in Memphis that this was the first time she'd enjoyed shopping since her husband died.
- And so many more.

It hurts to see the lack of confidence of others and to feel their pain. It hurts to remember my own pain and lack of confidence in the years when I tried so hard to try on one "fashion mask" after another in a pitiful attempt to fit in. But those days are behind me and I hope they are for you, too.

It's such a waste of time to try to be like everyone else when you have within you everything it takes to be so much more—uniquely you! It's been there all the time—that's the penultimate HOAX!

I often think of a charming woman I met after a show in Tennessee. She sent me some delicious homemade candy with a note that said:

> *"Here's a little sweet Southern energy booster. I'm sure you get tired traveling so much, but I think what you're doing is very good for women. I'll say a prayer for you."*

I'll say one back—for all of us.

WARDROBE COLORS

SUBDUED	VIBRANT	PASTEL

COOL

SUBDUED	VIBRANT	PASTEL
black	lemon yellow	pale pink
brown	royal blue	mauve
navy	hot pink	ice green
charcoal gray	white	ice yellow
maroon	clear red	pale seafoam
forest green	turquoise	baby blue
purple	clear green	pale gray

WARM

SUBDUED	VIBRANT	PASTEL
medium/ dark brown	bright yellow/ gold	coral/ peach
dark olive	orange	pale blue
burgundy	hot aqua	lavender
taupe	tomato soup red	muted jade
deep mustard	periwinkle	mustard
rust	cream/ winter white	olive green
teal blue	lime green	camel/beige